Exploring Montana's
PIONEER MOUNTAINS

TRAILS AND NATURAL HISTORY OF THIS HIDDEN GEM

PHOTOGRAPHY AND TEXT BY LEROY FRIEL

ISBN 13: 978-1-59152-133-4

Published by Leroy Friel

Front cover photo: Crescent and Abundance Lakes
from the pass above Teacup Lake, July 21, 2009.

Back cover photo: Torrey Mountain, June 10, 2013.

You may order extra copies of this book by calling
Farcountry Press toll free at (800) 821-3874.

s✹eetgrassbooks
a division of Farcountry Press

Produced by Sweetgrass Books.
PO Box 5630, Helena, MT 59604; (800) 821-3874; www.sweetgrassbooks.com.

The views expressed by the author/publisher in this book do not
necessarily represent the views of, nor should be attributed to,
Sweetgrass Books. Sweetgrass Books is not responsible for the
content of the author/publisher's work.

Printed in the United States of America.

28   27   26   25   24   3   4   5   6   7

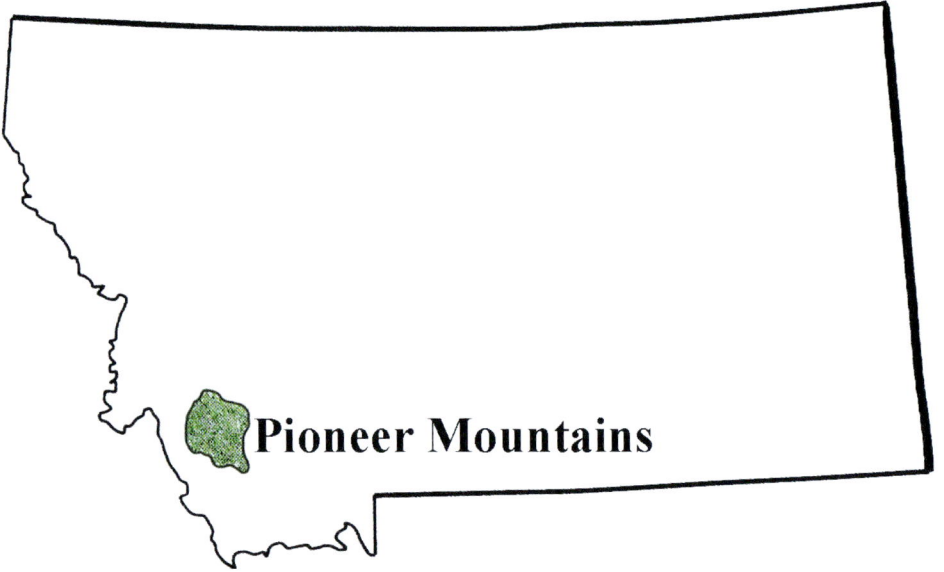

Pioneer Mountains

TABLE OF CONTENTS

✳

✳

INITIAL INSIGHTS

✳

PURPOSE

This book is for anyone who:
- Likes to hike, fish, and camp at alpine lakes.
- Has some historical connection to the Pioneer Mountains.
- Makes all or part of their living from the mountains.
- Spends time in the mountains.

ACKNOWLEDGMENTS

This book began at the suggestions of friends. They felt that I had sufficient information of the trails, lakes, and mountains to write a book; I was presumptuous enough to believe that I could succeed. I have hiked to many lakes in the mountains surrounding Butte, Montana, and in the early 1990s, I began to take pictures of those lakes. Writing this book has added to my several other hobbies.

I appreciate the numerous friends who helped, proofread, and encouraged this group project. I especially appreciate my good friend Dr. Paul Sawyer, professor emeritus of Montana Tech of the University of Montana, for his help identifying wildflowers.

SOURCES OF INFORMATION

While exploring these mountains, I have relied on topographic maps from Montana Bureau of Mines, maps from the U.S. Bureau of Land

Management, Google Maps, and Google Earth. Estimated coordinates for lakes and trailheads were acquired from Google Earth. Additionally, Google Earth and Google Maps display an abundance of pictures. I often print a contour map of my trip from Google Maps for my wife Patricia Ann.

For years I used *The Montanans' Fishing Guide* (with a volume for both east and west of the Continental Divide), and several maps to find the lakes. I tried to hike to as many different lakes as possible each summer. The updated western volume is called *The Montanans' Fishing Guide, Volume 1: Montana Waters West of the Continental Divide* by Dick Konizeski (Mountain Press, 2001, 416 pages). I like this book because of the short description of each lake, but at the present time, it may be difficult to find.

Much of the information on early mining can be found on websites. A small book, *One Man's Dream*, discusses the development of the Elkhorn Mine at Coolidge. The *Lake and Fish Directory* from the Beaverhead-Deerlodge National Forest describes the type of fish plus the depth and surface area of most lakes within the Pioneers. It is available as a pdf online, or from the national forest office at 420 Barrett Street in Dillon. *Wildflowers of Montana* by Donald Anthony Schiemann (Mountain Press, 2005, 306 pages) is helpful for identifying wildflowers of the Pioneer Mountains. Lastly, the Montana Historical Society and Beaverhead County Museum have been most helpful in providing details and dates of events in the Pioneer Mountains.

DISTANCES OF TRAILS

Tables in the back of this book include distance and hiking difficulty from the trailheads to the lakes.

Distances are deceptive in the mountains because we tend to estimate the distance based on sidewalk miles during the summer at lower elevations. We are used to walking, driving, or bicycling on smooth, dry, level ground. But when obstacles force us to walk around them, or the slope becomes steep and cliff-like at high elevations, then distance becomes secondary. Snowy weather can also lead to some danger on steep ground. A possible equation for estimating the difficulty for one trail mile is:

- Good path = 1.2 sidewalk miles
- No path through good timber or open range = 1.2 sidewalk miles
- No path through downed timber and brush = 1.5 sidewalk miles
- Good path with snow or snowshoes = 1.5 sidewalk miles
- 600 feet (183 m) steep elevation decrease = 1.0 sidewalk mile
- 500 feet (152 m) elevation gain = 1.0 sidewalk mile
- 400 feet (122 m) elevation gain above 9,000 feet (2,743 m) = 1.0 sidewalk mile

For example, hiking 1 mile through downed timber from 9,000 feet to 9,400 feet will feel like walking 2.5 miles on your neighborhood sidewalks.

WHEN DOES ICE MELT OFF LAKES?

Elevation is the most important influencing factor, but heavy winter snows and the amount of water flowing through the lake will also influence when the ice melts from the lakes. In the Pioneer Mountains melt generally occurs as follows:

Lakes at:
7,500 feet (2,286 m) - June 1
8,000 feet (2,438 m) - June 10
8,500 feet (2,591 m) - June 20
9,000 feet (2,743 m) - July 1
9,200 feet (2,804 m) - July 10

Chapter 1

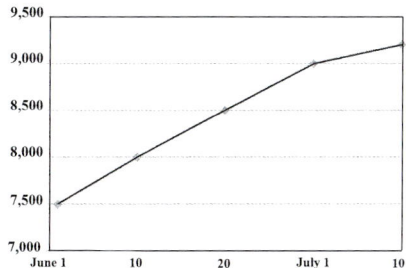

*

PIONEER MOUNTAINS PERSPECTIVE

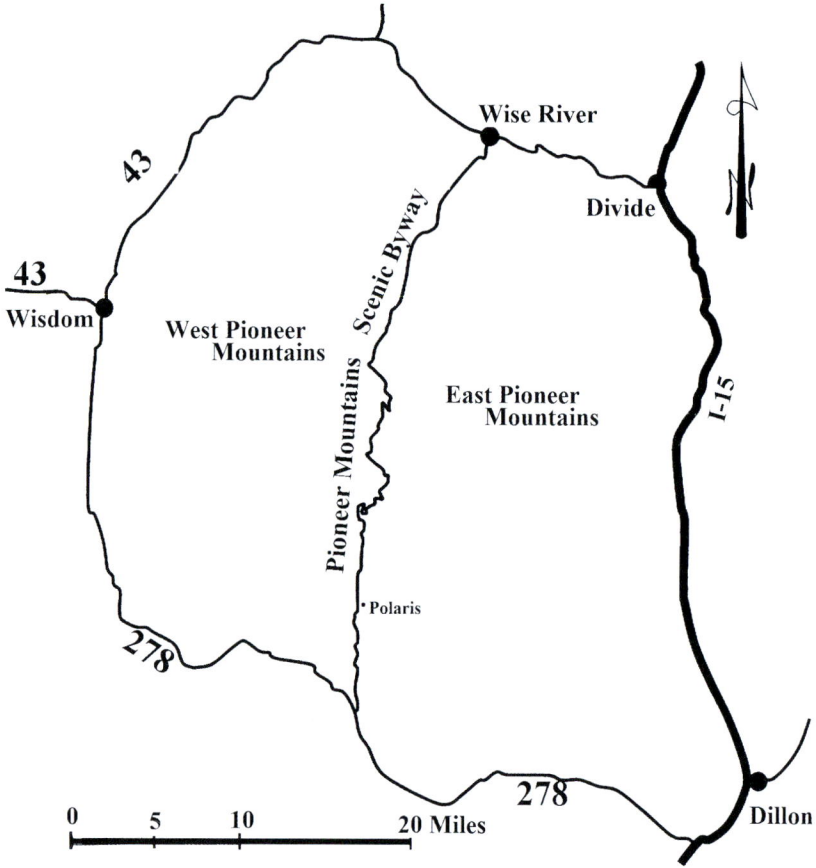

LOCATION AND OVERVIEW

The Pioneer Mountains are located in southwest Montana, just west of Interstate 15 and south of the Big Hole River and Montana Highway 43. The East Pioneer Mountains are east of the Pioneer Mountains Scenic Byway, which connects the towns of Wise River and Polaris. The West Pioneer Mountains are west of that road.

The East Pioneer Mountains include more than 50 peaks that exceed 10,000 feet (3,048 m); many of these remain unnamed. Many of the 59 lakes are situated at timberline with distinctive rocky slopes on one side. At lower elevations, the north-facing ridges have very thick brush and large trees, while at higher elevations very little vegetation clings to the steep, rocky, north-facing slopes. Snow hangs on north-facing rocky slopes well into July and August, leaving little time for vegetation to grow. In centuries past, glaciers carved deep lakes while permanent snow remained on the slopes. South-facing slopes at lower elevations remain dry and have thinner, smaller trees, making hiking through the timber easier. The East Pioneers host many mountain goats scattered over several mountain peaks. The East Pioneers may have fewer elk than the West Pioneers.

In the West Pioneer Mountains, about 20 peaks exceed 9,000 feet (2,743 m), which is 2,000 feet (610 m) lower than the highest peaks of the East Pioneers. Most of the 25 mountain lakes are in the timber and below timberline. Although some steep, rocky outcrops appear in the West Pioneer Mountains, and several of the drainages have downed timber, most of the mountains are rounded, often making for easier hiking. Fewer mountain goats live here. Because of predators, they do not survive as well in the timber. A greater elk population and ranching influence exist in the high meadows. Those who love horses will enjoy many trails in the West Pioneers. Many families have developed a kinship to certain areas, returning year after year to fish and elk hunt in the same area.

The four tallest peaks of the East Pioneer Mountains include Tweedy Mountain (11,154 feet, 3,400 m), Torrey Mountain (11,147 feet, 3,398 m), Granite Mountain (10,633 feet, 3,241 m), and Baldy Mountain (10,568 feet, 3,221 m). To climb Tweedy Mountain, the best approach is from Barb Lake just to the east for an elevation change of less than 2,000 feet (610 m), but some folks climb Tweedy Mountain from the Gorge Lakes to the north. To climb Torrey Mountain, the best approach is from Upper Bond Lake (Pond) just to the east of Torrey Mountain for an elevation change of 2,000 feet (610 m). Some folks climb Torrey Mountain beginning from Dinner Station Campground for an elevation gain of 4,000 feet (1,219 m). Granite Mountain can be climbed most easily from Granite Lake for an elevation change of 1,700 feet (518 m).

Baldy Mountain stands quite prominently at the south end of the East Pioneer Mountains. In winter, this large white-topped cone can be seen from most points on Montana Highway 278 from Dillon to Polaris. Baldy Mountain can be climbed best from Black Mountain Road to the south of the mountain. After turning off of Argenta Road, drive eight miles (12.8 km) on Black Mountain Road to where the road turns 270 degrees to the right. Baldy Mountain will be visible when looking down the road in one direction, and Black Mountain will be visible when looking down the road in the other direction. This location can be easily found on Google Earth at the approximate coordinates of 45°19'49"N 113°01'00"W as well as on USDA Forest Service maps. The road makes a sharp turn here; park your vehicle to begin the three-mile (4.8 km) climb with a 2,400-foot (732 m) elevation gain. The first objective will be to hike up the ridge to the saddle (45°20'38"N 113°01'00"W) between Black Mountain and Baldy Mountain. At the saddle, turn toward Baldy Mountain to find the established trail at timberline. The trail was developed many years ago when a fire tower was on the mountain, and this trail is faintly visible on both Google Earth and Google Maps. You can also take a three-dimensional visual tour around Baldy Mountain using Google Earth.

The two tallest peaks in the West Pioneer Mountains include Stine Mountain (9,490 feet, 2,893 m) and Odell Mountain (9,405 feet, 2,867 m). Stine Mountain rises just 900 feet (274 m) higher than Upper Grouse Lake. Odell Mountain's trail leads up to the peak from the south and from Sand Lake to the north. This trail on the south can be joined by the trail from Steel Creek, Stewart Meadows, or from Odell Lake. The total distance to the top of Odell Mountain from the Steel Creek Campground is 7.5 miles (12 km) with an elevation gain of 3,100 feet (945 m), while the distance from the parking area on Odell Creek to the top of Odell Mountain is slightly shorter, six miles (9.7

km), with an elevation gain of 2,200 feet (670 m). Using four-wheelers or trail bikes, visitors can drive up Lacy Creek to Lake of the Woods and hike from that point. On Odell Mountain, the trail is marked by piles of rocks and extends north for four miles (6.4 km) to Sand Lake. From the ridge, the beautiful view includes Elbow Lake and Baldy Lake to the east and the town of Wisdom to the west.

The south end of the East Pioneer Mountains becomes visible just west of Dillon. Baldy Mountain rises at the left side of the photograph below, with Black Mountain in line with Baldy Mountain and 1,200 feet (366 m) lower in elevation. Alturas No. 1 is just north of Baldy Mountain and Alturas No. 2 is northeast near the middle of the picture. The three mountain peaks connect via a high-elevation ridge. The peaks rise to nearly the same height, with Baldy Mountain only 18 feet (5.5 m) taller than Alturas No. 2. Highboy Mountain is between Alturas No. 2 and Tent Mountain near the photo's right edge, but Highboy Mountain is located several miles to the north. Torrey Mountain hides behind Tent Mountain, four miles (6.4 km) further north and 1,000 feet (305 m) higher than Tent Mountain. The tall peaks of the East

Baldy Mountain, May 11, 2011

Pioneer Mountains are 6,000 feet (1,829 m) higher in elevation than the ranchland around Dillon and north along Interstate 15.

Torrey and Tweedy Mountains can be seen from points just north of Dillon from Interstate 15 and from Montana Highway 41. Torrey Mountain is located at the left edge of the picture, while Tweedy Mountain is to the right. The prominent, unnamed peak near the middle of the picture is actually 600 feet (183 m) shorter than either Torrey or Tweedy Mountains. Upper Bond Lake is in the large bowl just east of Torrey Mountain with Torrey Lake over the ridge north of Torrey Mountain. Barb Lake is east of Tweedy Mountain in the large bowl formed by the Barb Mountain ridge. Barb Mountain appears as an east ridge of Tweedy Mountain.

Ice usually melts from most lakes by June 20, but above 9,000 feet (2,743 m) elevation, the ice can remain into early July. In late May and early June, snowshoes can be useful at higher elevations. Be careful of rocks that thunder down the steep slopes in small avalanches as the

Torrey and Tweedy Mountains, May 11, 2011

snow melts. Carry the snowshoes for the first part of the hike until deeper snow covers the path at higher elevations. July, August, and September are the best time for fishing. October is also usually a good time for fishing in the mountains, but snow adds chill to the already very cold winds sweeping across the lakes. The scenery sparkles beautifully during winter. Snowmobilers enjoy the Pioneer Mountains during the extended winter months.

The largest lake in the Pioneer Mountains, Agnes Lake, has a surface area of 109 acres (44 hectares). Tendoy Lake is the deepest lake at 100 feet deep (30 m). Green Lake is 92 feet (28 m) deep with a large surface area of 24 acres (10 hectares), providing a significant volume of water and good fishing on a consistent basis. Baldy Lake in the West Pioneer Mountains is 85 feet (26 m) deep with a surface area of 28 acres (11 hectares).

Total volume of water, lake surface area, lake depth, and flow of water through a lake all contribute to better habitat and better fishing. Grass and lily pads along the edges of a lake provide a home for insects and other water critters to hatch and live. In lakes such as these, the fish may grow bigger, but they are usually harder to catch. The fish may move to deeper water by mid-July, making the lake appear to be a dead lake, devoid of fish. Often fish flourish in large streams entering or leaving the lakes. Deep lakes tend to be cold, providing less food for the fish unless some part of the lake also has shallow water. Harsh winters often kill the larger fish, perhaps due to the lack of oxygen. As the ice melts in the early summer, many fish are thin and undernourished. The fish become more active a few weeks after the ice melts off the lake.

Tables in the back of the book describe lake and mountain characteristics. The name of the topographic map for each lake location is listed, and for some lakes, the surface area and depth are included. I provide my estimation of hiking distance, difficulty, and elevation change. I also include an assessment of the possibility of good fishing. The number of times that I have traveled to the lake indicates my appreciation for that lake. An abbreviated list of the height of mountain peaks is also included.

Few people venture on the trails or near the mountain lakes in the Pioneer Mountains. Some lakes with no fish and no trail receive very few visitors. It is exceptionally nice to walk solo through the mountains. Crescent Lake west of Melrose may be an exception, with horse traffic on trails and tents at lakeside on occasion.

Several longer hiking trips and extended fishing trips can be spliced together. One such trip could begin at Brownes Lake and continue past Waukena and Tahepia Lakes to Mono Campground. Other trips could cross drainages, such as a trip from Crescent Lake to Grayling Lake, or from Tendoy Lake to Gorge Lakes. Saddle horses encourage cross-country trips, especially in the West Pioneer Mountains, but on many cross-country trips, the horse should stay corralled as one climbs the ridge following mountain goat tracks. For the person who is well prepared, the lack of a trail, high mountain peaks, and steep ridges or serious weather should not be limiting factors. Those challenges provide campfire memories.

Brownes Lake and Kelly Reservoir can be reached by road. Even with road access, the lakes are not wheelchair accessible. A few lakes in both the East and West Pioneer Mountains can be reached using trail bikes or four-wheelers. Where motorized use is allowed, trails usually open after midsummer. When in doubt, consult a current travel map from the Beaverhead-Deerlodge National Forest. Most of the remaining lakes can be reached by horse or by mountain bike, and of course, by hiking boot. The lakes that would be difficult or unsafe for a horse include: Barb Lake, Glacier Lake, the upper two Grouse Lakes, Johanna Lake, Scott Lake, and Stone Lake East. A few folks appreciate those areas with no developed trails.

In addition to mule deer, elk, moose, sheep, and mountain goats, other animals such as coyote, badger, bobcats, spruce grouse, blue grouse, pika, and snowshoe hare roam the Pioneer Mountains. One time along the trail, I saw a pair of mink. On rare occasions, you may see a black bear, often with a brown coat. You will probably see tracks of both bears and mountain lions in the snow during the early spring and late fall, indicating that those two predators reside here. There may be an occasional grizzly in the Pioneer Mountains. On two occasions, I have seen large bear tracks that could have been grizzly tracks, and friends have told me that they have seen grizzlies. A friend of mine who bow hunts walked out of the timber just before dark when a very large bear entered the path ahead of him. The large bear stood in the path for a while and evaluated its prospects before returning to the trees to let my friend pass. At lower elevations, pronghorn and whitetailed deer graze.

A large variety of hawks and other large birds live in the Pioneer Mountains. It is nice to observe the silent glide of the great gray owl. Bald eagles fish in shallow alpine lakes and may nest close by. Early one morning as I approached a lake, I heard a loud splash. Hoping to see a moose, I quickly approached the lake and sat on a rock. An osprey struggled to move a large fish to shallow water. After finishing its meal, the osprey swam vigorously through the water to wash, and as it flew away, it shook its wings to shed excess water, leaving a spray of water hanging in midair.

The natural resources in the Pioneer Mountains include game animals, water, snow, grass, timber, and minerals. When it rains, snows, or hails in Montana, it is a pretty day, and the rain in May means a barn full of hay. Rain and snow provide grass in the mountains and hay in the lower valleys. With more water, more bench land could be irrigated and become more productive. As part of the Missouri River headwaters, snowmelt from the mountains flows downstream to help water Montana and the Midwest later in the summer. Western Montana does not have an abundance of large trees, but a few sizeable trees do grow in wetter drainages. The largest trees that I have seen in the Pioneer Mountains are in the Gorge Creek drainage south of the stream. The Pioneer Mountains contain deposits of gold, silver, copper, molybdenum, lead, and zinc. Mining may return sometime in the future.

Mosquitoes can be especially bothersome along the trails during summer. Open areas around lakes often have fewer mosquitoes. The colder weather of August and September also brings some relief from the pests. Many days, I have had wet feet from walking through wet grass, bogs, and snowbanks, or from fording streams. Even in July, a heavy frost may ice the meadows, and the exposed rocks in streams are often covered with a thin layer of ice.

Who owns the 1,400 square miles (3,626 square kilometers) of the Pioneer Mountains? As I look at the USDA Forest Service map, it appears that the Beaverhead-Deerlodge National Forest occupies 75 percent, the U.S. Bureau of Land Management manages 10 percent, the State of Montana presides over 5 percent, and private ownership possesses 10 percent.

Numerous mountain ranges throughout Montana and the Rocky Mountain region deserve attention. The Tobacco Root Mountains south of Whitehall, the Flint Creek Mountain Range north of Anaconda, and the Anaconda-Pintler Mountain Range west of Anaconda each has 50 or more lakes. Some of those lakes can be reached by truck and camper. The Beaverhead Mountains west of Wisdom also have numerous lakes.

POINTS OF INTEREST

The Big Hole River wraps around three-quarters of the Pioneer Mountains, tying them up in a nice package. Grasshopper Creek and the Beaverhead River line the south side of the mountains. The Big Hole, Beaverhead, and Ruby Rivers merge near Twin Bridges to form the Jefferson River. These three rivers form the upper headwaters of the Missouri River.

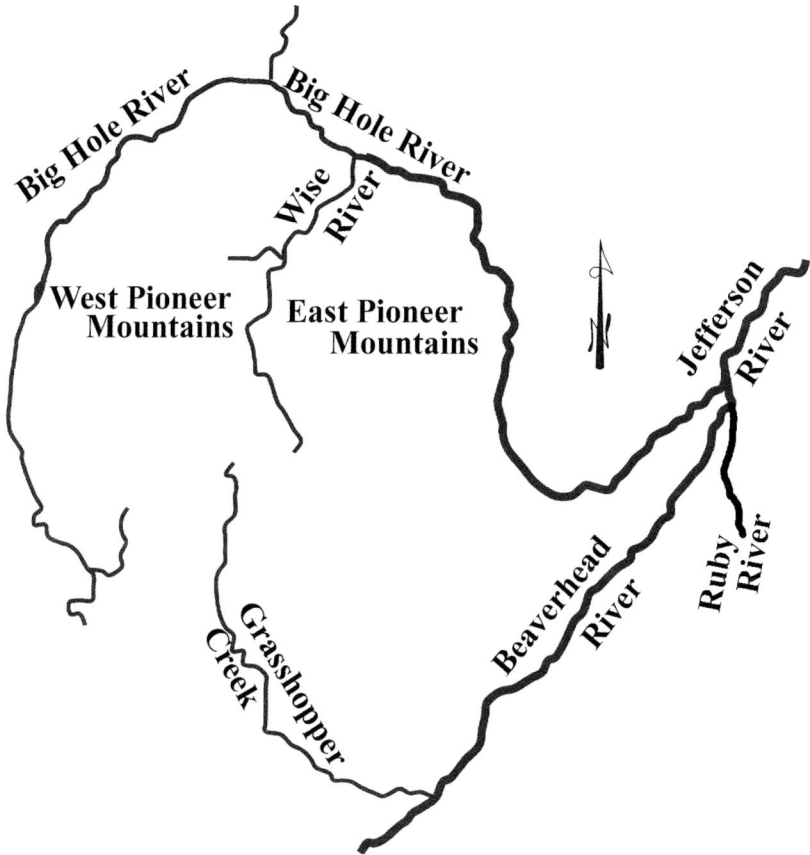

The Big Hole River is an exemplary fishery and a significant economic asset to southwest Montana. Because of its value, this river deserves extra attention, care, nurturing, and love. Many people have moved into the Big Hole Valley as their primary or secondary home. More people camp and fish along the Big Hole River each year than access all of the lakes in the Pioneer Mountains. Many people float and fish using McKenzie River boats or rubber rafts during the salmonfly hatch in June and follow that hatch upriver later in the summer.

The Big Hole Valley is a 2,800-square-mile (7,250 sq. km) watershed supporting many large working ranches, especially in the upper valley.

A scenic day's drive begins at Melrose and continues northwest and counterclockwise to Wise River, Wisdom, Jackson, Bannack, and back to Dillon. Use the internet and www.visitmt.com to investigate points of interest. Southwest Montana attracts numerous local and out-of-state visitors each year.

Fifty to 100 years ago, far more people lived in the Pioneer Mountains than now. Many old log cabin foundations indicate that homesteaders, prospectors, and solitude seekers lived in nearly every part of the mountains. At that time, crews clear-cut far more timber and built trails, roads, and small dams. Fish were planted in most of the alpine lakes by the late 1800s, though record keeping did not begin until 1931. Mining possibilities were extensively prospected, pursued, and mined.

Mining, primarily in the East Pioneer Mountains, started during the mid-1860s. Some historic mining locations include Bannack, Argenta, Farlin, Trapper Creek, Quartz Hill, and the town of Coolidge. Argenta had the first smelter in Montana in 1866. Thousands of prospectors flooded into these areas in the late 1800s and departed as quickly when they did not find the promised easy riches. A few did become rich, but most prospectors barely made a living or went broke trying. Rich deposits of gold or copper were found in Bannack, Virginia City, and the Butte copper mines. Bannack, now a ghost town and state park, celebrates the boom-and-bust era.

The town of Coolidge is 25 miles (40 km) south of the town of Wise River. From Wise River to Mono Campground, 18 miles (29 km) of paved road lead to Mono Campground where 7 miles (11 km) of good dirt road wends to the parking lot, located 0.5 mile (0.8 km) from Coolidge. Years ago, the drive to the town traveled over a much more difficult road, but one could drive up to the town. The initial ore discovery was made in the mid-1870s and several small ventures worked the district until William R. Allen (Lieutenant Governor of Montana from 1909 to 1913) began buying up claims in 1911. Allen and his partners made a considerable investment of money and time in the Elkhorn mining venture. They developed the mine, built a town, constructed a large concentrator, and laid a 38-mile (61 km) narrow-gauge railroad to the town of Divide. Telephone and electricity extended to the town of Coolidge. The town also had a post office, a school, and a company store, but no church. Mining discontinued about 1935, and the remains of the railroad were removed by 1940. Attempts were made to develop the mine as late as 1945.

Remnants of the town and the foundation for the large mill remain standing. The grand tipple stood through the mid-1990s when the following picture was taken.

Coolidge Mill, August 26, 1995

A few folks remember living in Coolidge for a year or so. The following was written by Adele Sawyer:

> *Times have changed drastically since the 1940s. To visit the mine of Coolidge, even though most of the buildings have fallen in, gives*

you a sense of just how primitive living could be: the isolation, the weather, the distance, etc.

In 1941, I was just a small tot when I lived at Coolidge the first time, and we lived in the hotel. On December 7, 1941, my grandfather, Andy Pyle, and my dad, Coulter Given, had made a trip with horses and a sled to bring food and news to the miners who spent the winter putting in the mine shaft and cutting wood at the sawmill for timbers and for the houses. Most of the miners lived in the bunkhouse at the upper mine.

The second time I lived at Coolidge, I was a little older, maybe three or four. We lived in Lieutenant Governor Allen's house. My dad worked for the mine at that time.

Then in the late 1940s, my dad, Coulter Given, worked for the mine again. They had hopes of starting it up again. Dad was trying to get some huge generators working at the mine, and we spent all summer up there. We lived at Polaris, and Dad made the trip to Coolidge every day. My brother Jim and I went with Dad while he worked. We weren't much help; we mostly explored. One of our favorite pastimes was walking around on the 2x4 rafters. We were a long way off the floor. But we were like the rats that scurried around. No fear!

The blow-down that went through that country in August of 1941 was a story that we grew up with. Perry Goodwin and his wife were living at Coolidge at the time. After a night of ferocious winds, Perry grabbed his saw (not a power saw) and was going to clear the road. He could see a short distance before the curve and could see a few trees. When he got to the curve, he could see the destruction and knew that he would need help.

Adele Sawyer grew up in Polaris. Her great-grandfather discovered Elkhorn Hot Springs and was involved in some of the early mineral discoveries in the area. She and her family have had a lifelong attachment with the area in both mining and ranching.

The Pettengill Dam (Pattengail) or Wise River Dam washed out June 14, 1927, after nearly 30 years of service. The washout claimed the lives of four people, damaged the towns of Wise River and Dewey, washed out a few miles of the narrow-gauge railroad track to the town of Coolidge, washed out several bridges, and damaged the dam and water supply at the Divide pump station. Montana Power Company constructed the reservoir in April 1900, and carried the legal liability for the damage. Beaver had closed the 42-inch (1.1 m) drain pipe, and water spilled over the emergency spillway. Seepage through the very fine sand fill in the south end of the dam caused the failure and permitted an enormous amount of water to be released. Some of the dam still exists one mile (1.6 km) up from the confluence with Wise River. Drive the Pettengill Road for two miles (3.2 km) to the stream to find the old dam.

The first bridge over the Big Hole River was the Brownes Bridge located six miles (9.6 km) downstream from Melrose. Fred Burr and James Minesinger constructed the toll bridge in late 1862 and early 1863. The multi-span timber, king-post truss was located slightly up-stream from the present steel truss. Joseph A. Browne purchased the bridge in 1865 and managed it as a toll bridge until his death in 1909. Browne lived on a ranch near the bridge. Madison and Beaverhead Counties assumed joint ownership of the bridge in 1911. The steel truss was constructed during the winter of 1915, and part of the timber truss washed out soon after the steel truss' completion.

The Glendale Smelter was seven miles (11 km) west of the town of Melrose. The smelter, constructed in 1875, operated for 15 years until 1890, when silver mining became less profitable. The smelter and town began to dismantle in 1900. Today only the square smelter stack and a few other buildings remain. Attached is a view of the smelter stack looking south.

The 23 antique charcoal ovens rest along Canyon Creek, 12 miles

Glendale Smelter Stack, June 17, 2010

(19 km) west of Melrose, and they provide a good picnic lunch spot. To visit the Canyon Creek Charcoal Ovens, drive west from Melrose or drive up Quartz Hill Road from the town of Dewey through Vipond Park, 15 miles (24 km) from Dewey. The road from the top of the hill above the charcoal ovens is steep, rough, and one lane for two miles (3.2 km). Following is a view of some of the charcoal ovens with recent snow covering the mountainside in mid-June.

Six charcoal ovens remain in Sucker Gulch (approximate coordinates 45°37'09"N 112°51'12"W) on the hill above the Glendale Smelter Stack, and one charcoal oven sits just north of Kelley Reservoir. The six charcoal ovens in Sucker Gulch are in poor condition, but some of the ovens still have wood laid, ready to be fired. Workers probably loaded charcoal on sleds and slid down the steep hill to the Glendale Smelter. To hike to these six charcoal ovens, turn south through a gate one mile (1.6 km) east of the Glendale Smelter. Drive past the small cemetery up a rough road for three miles (4.8 km) to the deadend.

Charcoal ovens, June 17, 2010

Sucker Gulch is west around another steep drainage, a two-hour hike. These six charcoal ovens are visible from the air during winter.

Crystal Park is located 27 miles (43 km) south of the town of Wise River on a once-paved road, surfaced 25 years ago. Crystal Park was set aside by the USDA Forest Service and the Butte Mineral and Gem Club to encourage amateur rock collectors. Several years ago, I met a man who had just found a half-bucket of three-inch (8 cm) smoky quartz crystals. Finding that many large crystals in one nest, however, is rare since much of the ground has been reworked extensively. A person should be prepared to dig a deep pit to find good crystals. No camping is currently permitted at Crystal Park, but numerous campers stay in the area for a week at a time looking for those prized crystals.

Both rock and mountain climbers will find challenges in the Pioneer Mountains. One of the places that a technical rock climber could hang out over night on the side of a cliff would be just south of Tweedy Mountain. This cliff can be reached from Torrey Lake. Mountain climbers should wait until August when most of the snow will have melted. Even during midsummer, large rocks release from the top to crash down the mountains.

Following is a view of the east side of Sharp Mountain located west of Melrose with the peak of Tahepia Mountain just beyond. Notice the large barn-size "wart" on the upper face of Sharp Mountain. I suspect that the serious rock climber would enjoy the climb up the east side of this challenging mountain; the total climb is 1,500 feet (457 m) from the lake to the peak. Easier routes lead to climbs on Sharp Mountain from Waukena Lake and Tahepia Lake to the south or from the upper Trapper Creek drainage. Only experienced technical rock climbers who are prepared should attempt the climb up the face of Sharp Mountain.

There are two small caves just north of Argenta on private ground. Other caves may also exist in the Pioneer Mountains, but spelunkers are secretive to protect caves from damage.

East side of Sharp Mountain, June 18, 2013

Numerous maintained and unmaintained campgrounds exist in the Pioneer Mountains. Public and private camping areas are found along the Big Hole River and along the Wise River drainage.

The old stage route from Bannack to Melrose and then on to Deer Lodge is shown in the map on the following page. Travel up Hangman's Gulch past the cemetery and Road Agent Rock to the divide and then on to the Rattlesnake Ranch. Continue up through

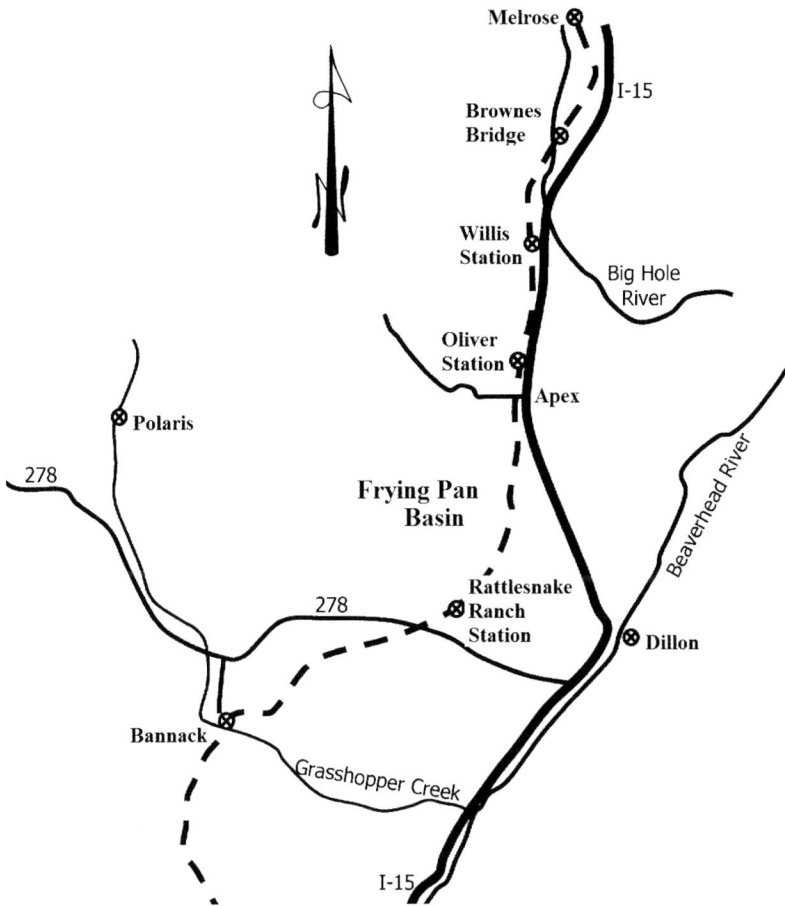

Frying Pan Basin to cross Birch Creek past the Oliver Station, Willis Station, and to Brownes Bridge.

Road Agent Rock north of Bannack was one of the places that road agents held up the stagecoach as its team of horses or mules struggled up the steep slope. When the stage stopped to rest the horses, the road agents would come out from behind the rock to rob the passengers and stage. For their deeds, several of the road agents were hanged by vigilantes in early 1864. Road Agent Rock is located two miles (3.2 km) north of Bannack on a steep, rough trail.

Hangman's Tree is actually a large stump and the remains of a

Road Agent Rock, September 1, 2010

large Douglas-fir tree. It is located three miles (4.8 km) past Farlin or 10 miles (16 km) from Apex on Interstate 15. In the late 1800s, a horse thief was hanged here, giving the nearby stream the name of Thief Creek. The small Thief Creek soon empties into the larger Birch Creek.

Elkhorn Hot Springs is located 31 miles (50 km) south of the town

Hangman's Tree, June 24, 2011

of Wise River and 42 miles (68 km) northwest of Dillon. The lodge and several cabins were built in the 1920s. Nearby attractions include the hot springs, extensive cross-country ski trails, downhill skiing at Maverick Mountain, and snowmobiling.

Jackson Hot Springs is located in the town of Jackson, 100 miles (161 km) southwest of Butte and 50 miles (80 km) northwest of Dillon on Montana Highway 278. The hot springs, lodge, and motel are located at the center of town.

Big Hole National Battlefield is 10 miles (16 km) west of Wisdom on Montana Highway 43. In August 1877, the Nez Perce under the leadership of Chiefs Joseph and Looking Glass, fought against the U.S. Cavalry during their failed attempt to escape to Canada. A visitor center and walking path at the park offer details and insight into the battle.

Two places provide exceptional views in the East Pioneer Mountains, and these two points are reasonably easy to access. The panoramic view from near Chain Lake (45°24'48"N 113°00'21"W) overlooking

Torrey Mountain from the west, September 30, 2006

the basin west of Torrey Peak features several lakes, including Pear Lake. To get to Chain Lake, hike past Minneopa Lake (45°23'33"N 112°57'50"W), Tent Lake, and Twin Lakes to Chain Lake, which is just west of Tent Mountain. The distance is four miles (6.4 km) with an elevation gain of 1,600 feet (488 m). Horses can probably travel for most of the distance except for the last 100 yards (91 m).

The second exceptional viewpoint is from above Hopkins Lake and the town of Coolidge. To get to this point (45°27'26"N 113°02'16"W), walk up the Dingley Creek drainage to the upper end of the valley. Horses can manage the climb to just below the ridgeline.

Hopkins Lake, August 2, 2011

The view from Proposal Rock east of Wisdom is also exceptional. The surrounding 360-degree view includes snowcapped mountains nearly year-round. Wisdom is to the west in the expansive upper Big Hole Valley, with the Beaverhead Mountains further west to the Idaho border. On the north, the Anaconda-Pintler Mountains extend across the horizon. The West Pioneer Mountains line the eastern horizon.

Below is a view of Wisdom from near Proposal Rock looking west across the upper Big Hole Valley to the Beaverhead Mountains.

Wisdom, June 26, 2010

Proposal Rock can be reached by a rough, steep road, five miles (8.0 km) east of the Wilson Cemetery, which is located five miles (8.0 km) north of the town of Wisdom. For another approach to Proposal Rock, walk through the timber from the trailhead to Lily Lake West. The trailhead is (45°36'31"N 113°20'14"W) located up the steep road north of the parking area near the Steel Creek Camping area. Total distance from the trailhead to Proposal Rock is four miles (6.4 km) with an elevation gain of 1,000 feet (305 m).

Proposal Rock can be seen in the distance from near Wisdom. Following is a much closer view of Proposal Rock.

Proposal Rock, June 26, 2010

BACKCOUNTRY SAFETY

Most of the time few real dangers exist in the mountains, but the consequences of an accident could be dire. The most probable accidents involve a twisted ankle or a fall. Avoid rock fields, talus slopes, and steep avalanche chutes when possible. Occasionally, large rocks hurl down avalanche chutes followed by a swarm of smaller rocks.

Protect your eyes while walking through timber, especially while off trail at night. Wear a wide-brimmed hat and look down at the ground rather than looking forward. Use your hands and arms for additional protection.

Avoid hiking beyond your capability. Those who are in poor health, not used to hiking, and not used to hiking at high elevations should be especially careful.

Many roads are not regularly maintained, making travel difficult. Good judgment would encourage a person to find a parking spot and walk instead of driving a new truck over rock piles and rough spots.

Avoid ridgetops during lightning storms and whenever there is potential for lightning. The peaks attract most of the serious lightning strikes, and a person will usually be safe at slightly lower elevations, especially while in the timber. Avoid wearing a metal pack frame or using metal walking sticks when above timberline.

Cross snow bridges over running streams only when necessary, with snowshoes spreading out the load. The long, steep caverns carved by streams under the snow can be especially dangerous if one is trapped in the cavern. Stay off lake ice during early summer; springs entering the lake under the ice may make the ice thin and uncertain. Snowmobilers or skiers should avoid traveling onto unsafe slopes and potentially producing a dangerous avalanche. Avalanche forecasts, avalanche-safety classes, and rescue shovels, probe poles, and transceivers are worth the expense for winter backcountry travelers.

During spring runoff, stream temperatures can be just above freezing, and the flows extremely powerful. A person could be quickly carried downstream to rocks and more danger. Hypothermia is possible when wet or tired, even when temperatures are mild. Avoid getting wet either from falling into water or from cold rain and hailstorms. Take extra clothing and supplies in a backpack. It is worth the weight to take an extra coat, space blanket, fire starter, extra food, flashlight, knife, compass, GPS unit, map, and perhaps a rope. Carry at least two knives, two flashlights, and two ways of making a fire.

Avoid building campfires during summer. Strong winds can reignite even a small spark long after you've gone. When a fire is needed, make sure to put it out cold, stirring the coals and wetting them thoroughly. Any fire should be in a location that can be easily contained and eliminated. Avoid traveling near wildfires, and report such fires if appropriate.

Normally, wild animals are not a problem. Pet dogs may draw an irate moose or bear back to the pet owner. Wild animals need their safe space. Avoid getting close to moose with calves and bears with cubs. Never approach a sick animal since it may have rabies. Pepper spray is probably the best defense, but some folks prefer a heavy pistol. Pepper spray was not available when I first began hiking in the mountains. Now it is available, reliable, and highly recommended. I have carried nothing more than a knife and a fishing pole except when hunting. Rattlesnakes live only at lower elevations along the rivers and some streams. In general, cell phone reception is poor in the mountains and should not be relied upon.

SECRET LAKE

Many people have been going back to a particular lake for several years, and they feel that lake is their special lake. I apologize to those that feel that this book reveals some of their secrets, but following is a photo of an interesting lake that I found. Getting to this lake requires a two-hour drive up a steep, rough, four-wheel-drive road followed by a four-hour hike from the trailhead. The long hike is well worth the effort, however, since one side of the lake has a nice, sandy beach. Large, hard-to-catch, eight-pound cutthroat trout often cruise near the shore.

At that lake, for a moment, a large cutthroat male swims close to shore, slowly and with some effort because of its size. The head seems even deformed with the large hooked jaw and the change in slope where the head joins the body. The fish is looking for its morning meal of freshwater shrimp and will take little else. It swims past an old rotting tree trunk and water lilies to disappear in the depths. But that trout was there, and we saw it. It would be a shame to kill such an ancient fish. It appeared to have white whiskers that seemed to drag on the bottom as it swam away.

Secret Lake

Where is this lake? Does it really exist? Are you kidding? Yes, of course, it is a real lake, a little west of Melrose. No! It is a little farther on. Those who know where this lake is will not tell, and neither will I.

ALONG THE TRAIL

The following are some of the encounters and mishaps that have happened as I have spent time in the mountains.

More than 35 years ago, I waded across the Big Hole River at Fishtrap Creek to retrieve my elk. After making several trips with a backpack, I drove home with wet feet and wet pants in a cold truck. A year later, I walked across the river on thin ice. At midway across, I punched through and stood in waist-deep frigid water. The situation was fairly safe, but interesting. I still hunt elk in a serious way, but with less energy. I usually hunt closer home.

One day in early June, I was hiking to Bobcat Lakes from the trailhead on Lacy Creek. After hiking for two hours, I had stopped to eat a sandwich. While sitting on an old rotten stump, I noticed a white hawk in a tree nearby. This hawk seemed to have an injured foot, and

I talked to it for a little while before it flew away. As I got up to leave, I realized that I had been sitting by a half eaten red squirrel. I had been sitting by the hawk's lunch. Farther up the hill, the snow became deeper and had several very large bear footprints. The snow was soft and melting, but the bear tracks were still exceptionally big and a little concerning. By that time, I had put snowshoes on and continued to climb the hill to the Bobcat Lakes. Ice still covered most of the lakes, and the fishing was very poor at the first lake. There had been a small avalanche near the second Bobcat Lake. I continued over the small pass in soft snow to Grassy Lake on the other side of the mountain. As I returned back over the ridge above Bobcat Lakes #3 and #4, I noticed some red snow along the ridge top. That snow is red because of the red algae growing in low spots on top of the snow. Some folks say that the red snow tastes and smells like watermelon but may make one sick. Also, it may be noted that the algae often attracts microscopic bugs and worms. In that case, one could have some protein with the toxic red snow.

One year in mid-July, I hiked to Bobs Lake. I parked the truck at the end of the road west of Vipond Park and hiked over the ridge south of Sheep Mountain into the Sheep Creek drainage. First I visited Bobs Lake and then climbed the ridge above the lake. The ridge is between the upper Sheep Creek drainage and the upper Boulder Creek drainage to the south. For some reason, my energy level was depleted; perhaps I had not consumed enough water. I had also walked a long distance and had climbed about 2,500 feet (762 m) to that point. I slowly struggled up the ridge. I had intended to walk down to Black Lion Lake, but I realized that I did not have the energy to accomplish that task. I took pictures and turned toward the truck several miles away.

I was on the upper slope of Black Lion Mountain North. I could have dropped back down into the Sheep Creek drainage or climbed up over Black Lion Mountain, but my energy was essentially gone. I decided to cross the side of the peak, traversing several steep avalanche chutes with very steep slopes. I crossed those dangerous places as quickly as I could to avoid falling rocks. Finally, I was near the end of the steep, rocky slope and near firm ground again. With confidence I stepped out quickly, but I stepped on a rock that rolled and threw me down the steep slope. I instinctively tucked and rolled as I had in football years ago. I think that I rolled three times before I threw out my arms to stop just before a 10-foot (3.0 m) drop off. My back hurt a little and my head bled, but I had no apparent broken bones. I could get up and walk. The rocks were as big as an office desk, and my glasses and hat were down in between those rocks. I slowly walked over to firm ground and sat down for 15 minutes before slowly walking back to the truck. Later the doctor confirmed that I had broken three ribs, but I felt very fortunate that I had not gotten hurt more seriously.

Following is a view of the steep slope just north of Black Lion Mountain. This photograph was taken the first week of July, and the

North Slope of Black Lion Mountain, July 8, 2010

hill still had considerable snow. I had crossed this slope later in the summer. From this picture, it appears that it would have been safer and easier to climb up and over the peak. I have been on the east side of Black Lion Mountain North several times because of the grand views and the search for wildflowers.

One of my favorite hiking partners was Wan, a Chinese national from the country of Malaysia. He was a student in Petroleum Engineering at Montana Tech of the University of Montana. His mother had made him promise that he would be especially careful of bears because she had only one son. One early spring, we crossed a small bear track in soft snow. I explained to him the difference between a black bear track and a grizzly bear track. Later I noticed that he constantly looked back up the trail, and I asked him what he was looking for. He said, "The next time I come up here, I will bring a gun." Another time as we were walking around a steep ridge, he asked me if I had a compass. I stopped and took the compass out of my backpack and showed him. When I put the compass away again, he said, "Aren't you going to keep the compass out?" I reassured him that I knew our location. From the ridge, I pointed out several vantage points and pointed to where the truck was parked three miles (4.8 km) distant over the hill.

I twisted my ankle the first time that I hiked into Torrey Lake. The lake is nine miles (14 km) from Mono Campground, and it takes four hours to walk that distance. After walking for four hours, my ankles were swollen slightly. When I stepped on a sloping rock, my right ankle twisted, and I twisted my ankle a second time before I could get to firm ground. It took seven hours to return to the truck at the trailhead. At home, I stayed off my feet for a week and was on crutches for another two weeks, not an experience that I want to repeat.

On my way to Hopkins Lake near the town of Coolidge, I stepped out on what appeared to be solid ground. I sank into a small, deep mud hole, chest deep. I thought that happened only to people in the movies or the comic strips but not in real life, and certainly not to me. I continued my hike to Hall and Hopkins Lakes. I used the drip dry method for the rest of the day and was almost comfortable by the time I returned to the truck in the afternoon.

One morning, I prepared to walk from near Bond Lake to Deerhead Lake and then on to Upper Bond Lake. As I laced my boots, a large moose entered the clearing a short distance away. I quickly got my camera and began taking pictures. The moose continued to walk closer as it grazed along the hillside, and as the handsome animal slowly passed, I realized that it was either blind or nearly blind. It is also true that a large moose will often ignore people who are near.

Moose, August 12, 2010

One spring day west of Anaconda, I struggled and floundered in deep snow in an attempt to access a lake, but, finally exhausted, I admitted defeat and turned around. Snowshoes would have made the last half of the hike easy. Small bear tracks of a year-old cub had crossed my path a few times. On my way out, a huge pile of bear scat had been deposited in the place where I had rested earlier that morning. The large stack of bear scat would have made even a large bear proud, and it was far beyond the capacity of the smaller bear. I had to smile as I continued the hike to the truck. The she-bear was suggesting in her own way that I leave and not return. Big bears, especially, like to leave their calling card in the middle of the path or in the middle of the road.

In mid-June, I was in the Steel Creek area east of Wisdom looking for early wildflowers. I had hiked to Moose Meadows southeast of the campground. There I found a moose with a year-old calf. They watched me as I walked by with the wind in my favor. A little farther into the meadow, I saw two elk and something else that I supposed was another elk. All three animals began moving toward me and watching in the opposite direction. Apparently the two moose had gone that way, and the elk were moving away from the noise. As the two elk passed, I realized that the third animal was a black bear. It stopped at a tree and rubbed its back and continued past me to the timber. The bear stopped just inside the timber and glared at me as if to say, "Why are you bothering me!" I realized that I was a little close and backed off to continue my hike.

Black bear at Moose Meadows, June 9, 2010

Chapter 2

*

ENTERING THE EAST PIONEER MOUNTAINS FROM THE EAST SIDE

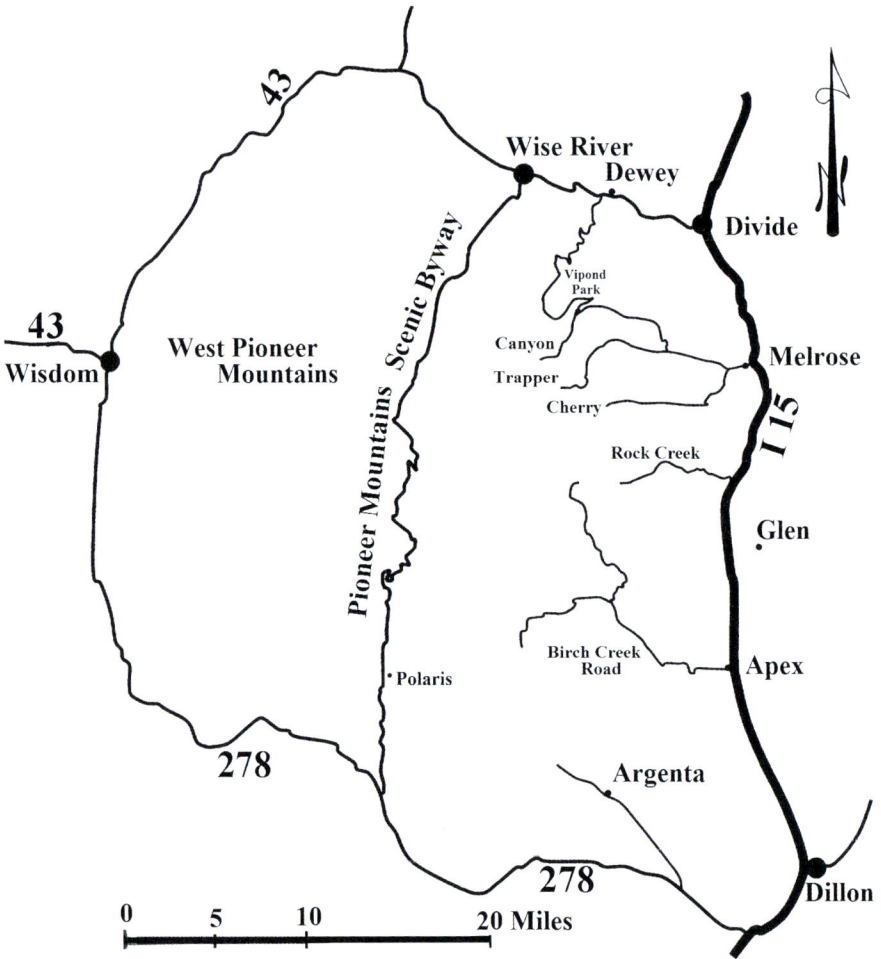

One half (45 of 89) of the Pioneer Mountains' lakes can be reached from the east side of the East Pioneer Mountains by roads and then by trails extending from Melrose, Glen, Apex, and Argenta.

ENTERING AT MELROSE

The drainages west of Melrose with alpine lakes include Canyon Creek, Trapper Creek, and Cherry Creek.

CATTLE GULCH LAKE AND TRUSTY LAKE

Cattle Gulch Lake and Trusty Lake are located at the east end of Vipond Park, and they are actually ponds or large, dependable springs. By midsummer, it's possible to drive to both lakes, but I have hiked to both of these lakes in early June from the ridge above the Charcoal Ovens on Canyon Creek. Often, hikers encounter some snow and wet hillsides at that time of year. Most of the hike winds through open meadows with outstanding views and many wildflowers, a very pleasant hike. Bighorn sheep may graze in the area. One time, I saw a badger cleaning dirt from her den.

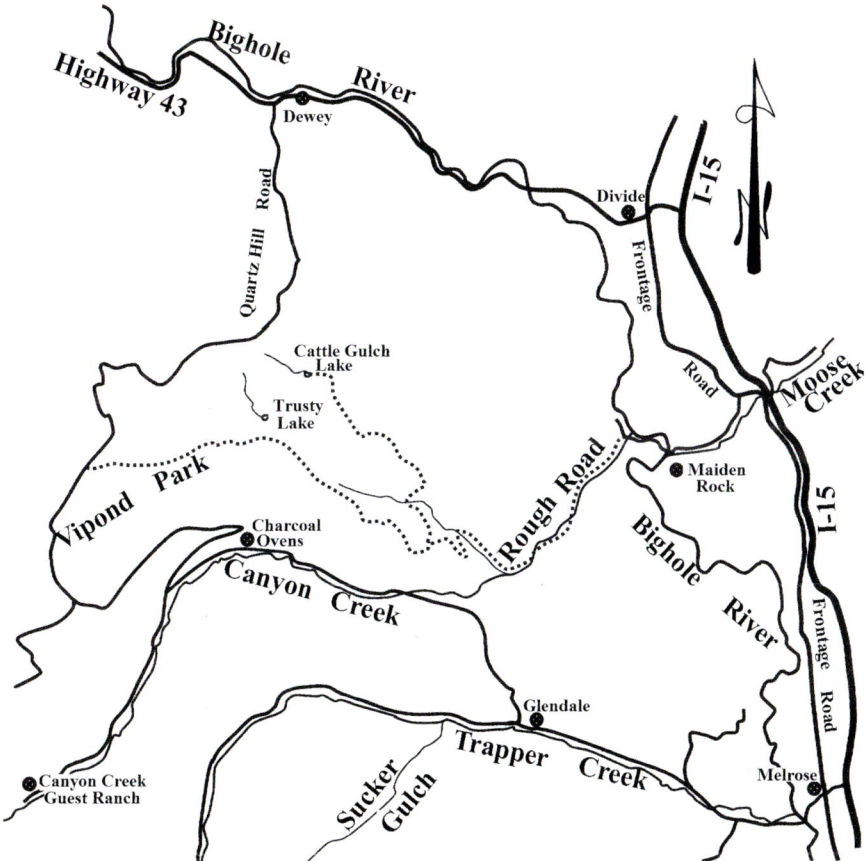

CATTLE GULCH LAKE

Cattle Gulch Lake (45°43'07"N 112°51'12"W) is located at the top of the hill at the east end of Vipond Park. A steep road 10 miles (16 km) from Maiden Rock may be used to access the lake.

TRUSTY LAKE

Trusty Lake (45°42'31"N 112°51'54"W) is near the top of the hill at the east end of Vipond Park. Trusty Lake is located near a road along the top of the ridge, three miles (4.8 km) east from Quartz Hill Road, which begins just west of Dewey. Also, a steep road or a four-wheeler trail branches from the road to Cattle Gulch Lake and connects to Quartz Hill Road. This is a challenging drive even in dry weather, but a great view provides photo opportunities as the road gains 3,000 feet (914 m) in elevation.

Trusty Lake with Sheep Mountain in the distant background. Pine beetles have killed many of the lodgepole pine trees, resulting in the reddish hue. June 12, 2009

CANYON CREEK CAMPGROUND

The total distance from Melrose to the trailhead on Canyon Creek is 18 miles (29 km). Drive west from Melrose up Trapper Creek Road for seven miles (11 km) to the old Glendale smelter, and then turn north over the hill to Canyon Creek past the historical charcoal ovens to the campground near the Canyon Creek Guest Ranch. Another approach is the drive up Quartz Hill Road from the town of Dewey to the trailhead.

For folks with horses, a stock unloading ramp and parking area is one mile (1.6 km) east of Canyon Creek Campground. A new bridge accommodates horse traffic with an accompanying trail extended to this unloading point. For those very few brave souls who drive in from the town of Dewey with a horse trailer, an additional lead truck would be nearly necessary because there is no place for two trucks to pass for a distance of two miles (3.2 km) on the steep hill. The second

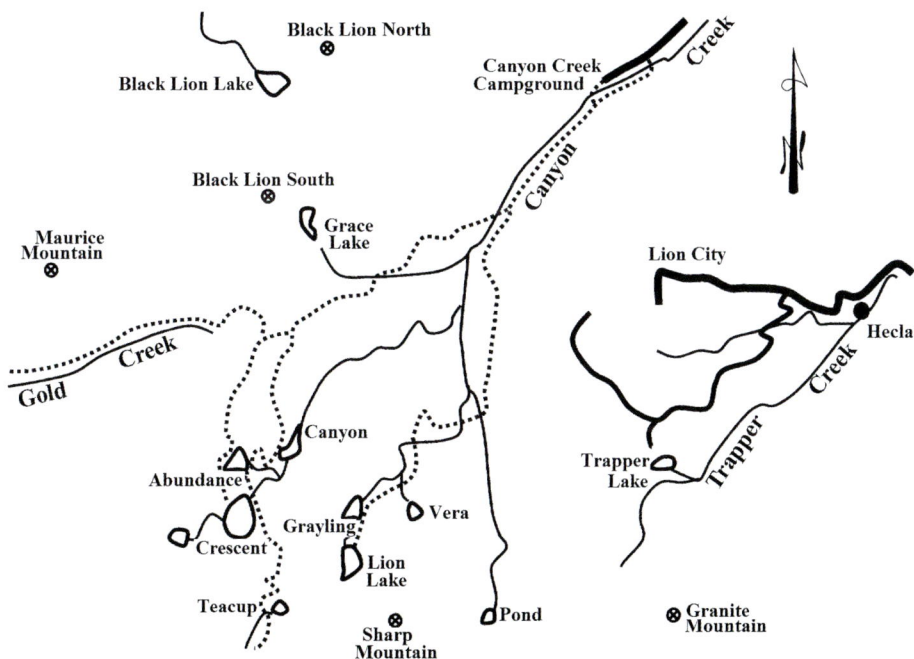

truck would lead interference down the narrow one-way road above the charcoal ovens.

As noted in the map on page 47, several lakes can be reached by hiking from the Canyon Creek Campground trailhead. Using Google Earth, note the approximate coordinates of the Canyon Creek Campground trailhead at 45°37'35"N 112°56'33"W.

CRESCENT, ABUNDANCE, AND CANYON LAKES

Crescent Lake (45°34'42"N 113°00'12"W) is at timberline in mountain goat country. Abundance Lake and Canyon Lake reside at slightly lower elevations. All three lakes harbor both large and small fish, but Crescent Lake has been the most productive. Canyon Lake is shallow and usually provides more small fish than you want to catch. Years ago when the limit was a generous ten fish per day, I often stopped by Canyon Lake on my trip out.

The lakes are 5.5 miles (8.9 km) and a 1,500-foot (457 m) climb from the trailhead on a good horse trail. Beginning from the campground, the trail crosses Canyon Creek on a reasonably good bridge. The trail branches after a mile (1.6 km). The upper (right) branch of the trail crosses Canyon Creek a second time and leads to Canyon, Abundance, and Crescent Lakes while the lower (left) branch of the trail leads to Vera, Grayling, and Lion Lakes. The second crossing of Canyon Creek is on a single log. This crossing would be dangerous and not recommended during the spring runoff since the water will be high, cold, and powerful. By the time the ice melts off Crescent Lake in late June, the runoff should be down to safer levels.

The trail branches again near the top of the mountain after three more miles (4.8 km) of walking. There is an old log cabin with two very nice streams before the branch in the trail. The right branch leads up the hill to Abundance and Crescent Lakes while the left branch leads around the hill to Canyon Lake. The two streams near the old cabin are both good places to refill a water bottle, using a filtration system, of course.

The steep trail leading up to Abundance and Crescent Lakes approaches the ridgetop overlooking the upper Gold Creek drainage. A short distance above the trail, a panoramic view of upper Gold Creek drainage includes Maurice Mountain in the background. The yellow, gravelly cliff with interesting geology drops off 800 feet (244 m) down to upper Gold Creek. Early one morning, I noticed a large elk on the steep hillside south of the drainage.

Abundance and Crescent Lakes receive horse traffic, and some groups camp for a week. The east side of Crescent Lake and the north side of Canyon Lake usually have abundant grass for horses. Canyon Creek Guest Ranch near the trailhead leads guests up to these lakes for the day at a modest fee. Those who cannot walk far can still have a high-mountain experience by sitting in the saddle.

The three lakes may be approached from the Wise River direction by way of Gold Creek; this is a good route for horses for a distance of seven miles (11 km), with an elevation gain of 2,700 feet (823 m). Also, a trail leads from Mono Campground past Teacup Lake and over the ridge to Crescent Lake. This trail is difficult and possibly dangerous for horses on the south side of the pass above Teacup Lake. Some trail improvement would be helpful for horses. Last, an old, unused trail leads downstream from Canyon Lake.

There are also two nice ponds near Crescent and Abundance Lakes. These two beautiful large ponds are at a higher elevation and are partially covered with ice into mid-July. Fish gather around the stream from the pond above Crescent Lake in early July. Perhaps the stream carries insects from the upper pond.

Mountain goats climb on the steep ridge above Canyon Creek. Binoculars help identify the billies and nannies.

Another view of Abundance and Crescent Lakes is from the ridge

The view from the outlet of Crescent Lake looking southwest. The main part of the lake is beyond the trees. June 30, 2007

above upper Gold Creek. Both lakes drain east over the hill to Canyon Lake. Looking south past Abundance and Crescent Lakes, you can see the small pass that leads down to Teacup Lake, with Alverson Mountain south of Schultz Lakes peeping up over the pass.

Abundance and Crescent Lakes, September 21, 2011

GRACE LAKE

Grace Lake (45°36'39"N 112°59'32"W) is northeast of the old log cabin on the trail to Crescent Lake. Leave the trail 0.5 mile (0.8 km) before the old log cabin and turn back north for a mile (1.6 km), gaining 500 feet (152 m) to Grace Lake. The lake is just east of Black Lion Mountain South but 1,500 feet (457 m) lower in elevation. Grace Lake is located in a very beautiful spot, but the lake is little more than a pond by September, home to an abundance of water critters. Fish do not survive in Grace Lake. I've found no well-defined inlet or outlet stream, and the lake may freeze nearly to the bottom during winter.

On page 52 is a view of Grace Lake from the ridge above the lake. For this view, I walked past the old log cabin to the top of the ridge overlooking the upper Gold Creek drainage. I then walked back northeast along the ridge to a small peak above and south of the lake. This provided a much better view of the lake from a higher elevation. As I climbed the small peak, I noticed horse droppings from several years before on the steep trail. There is a small, steep grassy drainage just north of the small peak that leads up from the south branch of Boulder Creek from the west and from Wise River.

Black Lion Mountain South looked so close that I could almost touch it, but the topographic map indicated that the peak was another 1,000 feet (305 m) higher than the pass or 1,500 feet (457 m) higher than Grace Lake. In the view of the lake, Black Lion Mountain North appears just over the ridge. Black Lion Lake is over the ridge to the west of Grace Lake between the two tall peaks. The best approach to Black Lion Lake is to climb up Boulder Creek from Wise River to the west. Both Black Lion Peaks stretch to about the same height in elevation with the south peak (10,432 feet, 3,180 m) reaching a little more than 10 feet (3.0 m) taller than the north peak. A high ridge connects these two peaks.

Even though it was a nice clear day, an exceptionally strong wind blew through the steep, grassy drainage as it funneled into the small pass. I dropped down over the ridgeline out of the strong wind to eat part of my lunch. At that time, I called my wife on the cell phone and told her that I missed her. Cell phone coverage is usually not available except at high elevations on the east side of the East Pioneer Mountains. Goat hooves left fresh imprints in the rock-hard, cemented dust on the ridge. Apparently the wind had betrayed me to the mountain goat, and it had walked around the ridge ahead of me and out of view.

I very carefully descended the steep ridge to take more pictures of the lake and of wildflowers. I returned to the trail a little more than a mile (1.6 km) away over the hill. Fifteen years earlier, I had stayed in the timber to intersect the trail at the bottom of the mountain near

Grace Lake, August 25, 2009

Canyon Creek. At that time, I had disturbed several elk, and the odor of elk was quite distinct and fresh in the timber.

GRAYLING, LION, AND VERA LAKES

These three lakes are at timberline in mountain goat country. Grayling (45°34'45"N 112°59'05"W) and Lion Lakes are the same size, the same depth, and are good producers of 12-inch (30 cm) fish. Lion Lake is quite beautiful, but Grayling Lake remains slightly warmer, providing the better fishing. Vera Lake is a small, shallow lake (three acres, one hectare) and may have no fish or an occasional large fish. This lake can be overfished easily. One spring, I found ten skeletons in Vera Lake of large fish that had died during the winter, but I also saw about 100 small, 4-inch- (10 cm) long fish. The fish may be reproducing in the lake, a good sign. The lakeshore at Vera proved quite clean with no fire rings or trash. One spring, I found an intact skeleton of a mountain goat along the lake edge with all of the bones and most of the hair still in place. Horse traffic frequents both Grayling and Lion Lakes.

In late May one year, I used snowshoes to hike into Lion Lake. It was useful to have waterproof boots at lower elevations since the trail was very muddy and slushy. At Lion Lake, 15 mountain goats with 5 kids appeared along the ridge south of the lake. Goats apparently have their babies about a week before elk or deer. The stream below the lakes cut through a five-foot-deep (1.5 m) canyon of snow.

The lakes are five miles (8.0 km) and a 1,600-foot (488 m) elevation gain from the trailhead at the Canyon Creek Campground. Half of that elevation gain occurs within the last mile (1.6 km). Vera Lake is just off the trail to the south. Also, the lakes are just over a steep ridge from Crescent and Abundance Lakes. Climbing the ridge from Crescent Lake and descending to Grayling Lake is far easier than going from Grayling Lake to Crescent Lake, since the ridge west of Grayling Lake is so very steep.

The views from the ridge east of Crescent Lake and east of Grayling Lake are outstanding. The climb east of Crescent Lake requires an elevation gain of 900 feet (274 m), while the climb east of Grayling Lake requires an elevation gain of 1,200 feet (366 m).

A large, fishless pond exists in the drainage just east of Vera, Grayling, and Lion Lakes. To get to this pond, leave the trail at about halfway in (approximately 45°35'23"N 112°57'47"W) and continue up the main drainage rather than crossing the stream on the trail to Grayling Lake. Hold a course near the stream since traveling up the hill on either side of the stream will be more difficult. The grass in the middle of the narrow drainage will probably be perfumed with elk droppings. Sharp Mountain is west of the shallow pond and east of

Lion Lake looking southwest in early July, by the outlet stream. Much of Lion Lake remained ice covered with a few winterkill fish near the shore. July 3, 2009.

Lion Lake. Teacup Lake is over the ridge southwest of Lion Lake but south of Crescent Lake.

THE PYGMY BITTERROOT

Written based on a climb above Vera, Grayling, and Lion Lakes.

Down on my knees and looking close, a pygmy bitterroot I suppose

*Seven pink petals flat to the ground with no stem,
no leaves and no other flowers around*

*Over there, fresh footprints and tufts of white hair,
evidence of the mountain goat pair*

*I climb the steep slope with yellow columbine,
mountain buttercups and stunted pine*

*The going is slow as upward I climb,
and I often look back to beg for time*

*Thick short grass clings tight to the ridge and
a small bird flits from a hole in the ledge*

*An hour later on the ridge crest a rest I take,
far below is Grayling Lake*

*The far side of the ridge drops dangerously steep with
a recent avalanche of tangled trees to a creek*

*Below and a little farther on is a large shallow pond,
a steep rocky ridge with Sharp Peak beyond*

*I lay for a while on a carpet goat drop matting;
resting, relaxing, thinking, dreaming, and napping*

*Dreaming of the mountains I love,
and also dreaming of climbing the jagged peak above*

*I may never return to this ridge,
drainage or to some of the lakes of this mountain range*

*As we get older, we think of those things
as we number our possible winters and springs*

*High elevation requires more effort on the hill.
I move slowly, deliberate, often stop, avoid a spill*

poem continued on page 56

I slowly descend the ridge to Lion,
leave for the day with no fish but a good time

I don't remember the three-hour walk on the trail,
nor the drive home, unimportant detail

I only remember the climb to the top, the flowers,
the strong wind and the jagged rock

Pink Pygmy Bitterroot, June 30, 2007

TRAPPER LAKE

Trapper Lake (45°35'04"N 112°55'57"W) provides a few small fish and is located in a beautiful spot at the head of Trapper Creek. Drive 15 miles (24 km) west of Melrose on Trapper Creek Road and then three miles (4.8 km) past the Hecla Mine buildings. The road leading to the lake branches south from the main road leading up to the Lion City Ghost Town. Trapper Lake is a short walk down a small hill from the road. The upper reaches of the road are best navigated in a four-wheel-drive vehicle.

Lion City Ghost Town contains several log houses in good condition. The alternate road that passes Trapper Lake continues up the mountain to well above the timberline. The high mountains provide several good above-timberline hikes and great views. The Trapper Creek drainage displays a wide variety of wildflowers since the elevation increases by more than 4,000 feet (1,220 m) from Melrose to the end of the road and more than 6,000 feet (1,829 m) to the tops of some mountain peaks. This area is also home to large mule deer, elk, and mountain goats. A large, beautiful brown-colored black bear crossed my path one summer. Both four-wheel-drive vehicles and four-wheelers use this area, though the road continues to deteriorate.

On one trip up Trapper Creek, a rubber boa wriggled in one tire track. Could someone explain why snakes like to sleep in the road? This creature reminds me of a 15-inch-long (38 cm) docile earthworm rather than a snake. Google Images will probably provide the only

Trapper Lake looking south. Green Lake is just over the mountain south of Trapper Lake. Granite Mountain (10,633 feet, 3,241 m) is the far peak in the background, and it is slightly taller (200 feet, 61 m) than the more prominent peak in the picture. June 23, 2009.

opportunity for most people to see a rubber boa, a non-venomous, nocturnal native. I gently moved the little snake to a safer place.

THE TRAILHEAD ON CHERRY CREEK

The trailhead on Cherry Creek is 20 miles (32 km) west of Melrose (45°35'32"N 112°50'42"W). Granite and Cherry Lakes drain into Cherry Creek, while Green Lake drains south to Rock Creek west of Brownes Lake.

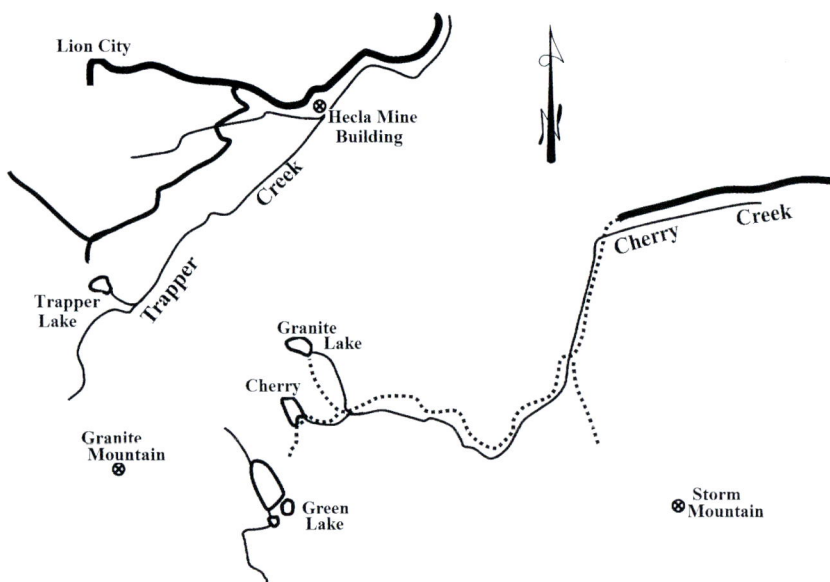

GRANITE, CHERRY, AND GREEN LAKES

Granite Lake (45°34'43"N 112°54'17"W) is shallow around the edges, providing easy wading while fly fishing. When I first visited the lake 30 years ago, I found numerous small brook trout, and even though I have visited the lake many times over the years, I have never fished the lake again. The lake has some deep water that holds stocked cutthroat

Granite Lake, September 18, 2009

trout. The last time that I visited the lake on my way to Trapper Creek, I noticed many fish rises on the surface.

The photograph of Granite Lake and the ridge that leads up to Granite Mountain to the west reveals the remains of a small snowdrift in mid-September. There must have been considerably more permanent snow in the East Pioneer Mountains 100 years ago.

CHERRY LAKE

Cherry Lake (45°34'21"N 112°54' 21"W), a lovely lake at timberline supports a few large fish. Throughout summer, four-wheelers travel to the lake, and some of those folks will stay overnight to fish. A small spring on the south-

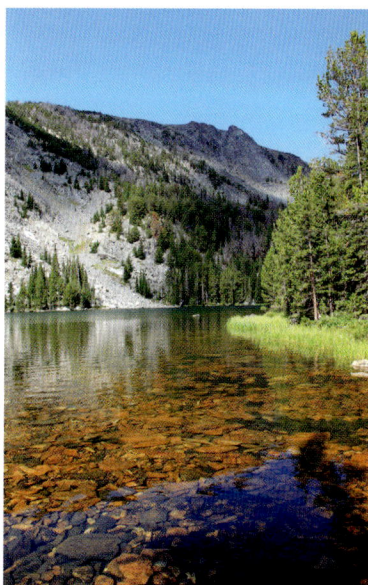

Cherry Lake, August 29, 2013

west side of the lake provides water for campers to filter. This view of Cherry Lake looks toward the northwest from near the outlet and the campsite. The ridge in the background is 700 feet (213 m) higher than Cherry Lake and is the same ridge that looms above Granite Lake. Granite Mountain is to the west of Cherry and Granite Lakes at an elevation gain of 1,700 feet (518 m). Green Lake is over the ridge to the south.

GREEN LAKE

Green Lake provides the most productive fishing of the three lakes because it is harder to access and because the lake contains a large volume of water. The approximate coordinates to the big toe of Green Lake are 45°33'49"N 112°54'21"W. Exceptionally deep at 92 feet (28 m), Green Lake features a large surface area with a good flow of water. The lake is shaped like a big footprint. The big toe on the southeast usually has large fish, while the small toe on the southwest has many small fish. The east side of the lake shoulders very large, house-sized boulders. These boulders are not only hard to climb but are dangerous. If a person fell into the water on the east side of the lake, there would be no way to get back out. It's not a place for children to fish. Because of the danger, one should avoid fishing from the boulders on the east side. My friends like this lake, and I usually have company here.

The lake is a hard lake to fish with flies since a good back cast is available only at the south end where a strong wind often blows. A few fishermen use float tubes and float from the north to the south end of the lake. This may be a good approach, but because of the lake's depth, the water remains exceptionally cold.

The photograph is taken from the big toe of Green Lake looking northwest. The main part of Green Lake is just over the rocks at the far side of this pond. In mid-August one year, the remains of snowdrifts in the form of a large "V" clung to Granite Mountain. From the Interstate

Big toe of Green Lake, August 20, 2011

turnoff at Melrose, Granite Mountain appears as a "gun sight" in the mountain range, and the other part of the mountain in the "gun sight" is the ridge above Cherry and Granite Lakes. The other peak in this picture is the same peak seen while looking south from Trapper Lake, which is almost directly north of Green Lake.

The trailhead to Granite, Cherry, and Green Lakes is on Cherry Creek, 20 miles (32 km) west of Interstate 15 at Melrose. Usually the dirt road is in good condition except when spring melt or a heavy rain slickens the clay base in some parts of the road. The second exception is that a four-wheel-drive vehicle is necessary for the last mile of travel. Otherwise the walk will be a little longer. The rough road continues to deteriorate, and one spot in the road is becoming steep and rocky. For a few years, there was a large tree across the road and a deep mud hole to cross, impeding a vehicle. The last time that I walked into Cherry and Green Lakes, the trailhead had been moved, requiring about one mile (1.6 km) of extra hiking.

The hike to the three lakes requires a five-mile (8.0 km) walk from the trailhead with a 2,200-foot (670 m) elevation gain. Granite and Cherry Lakes are accessible by motorbikes and four-wheelers. Granite Lake is just over a small hill to the north of Cherry Lake, a 30-minute walk through the woods. For a portion of the route, no trail exists. Green Lake is one mile (1.6 km) over a ridge to the south and west of Cherry Lake with no distinct trail for part of the way, since huge boulders block the entire east side of Green Lake.

To get to Green Lake, pick one of two options. The first is to leave the trail at the last bog below Cherry Lake and travel cross-country to the south end of the lake to the smaller boulders.The second option is to take the trail south of Cherry Lake and over the ridge. An old mule trail leads down the ridge to the south side of the lake, but this trail has essentially disappeared. Large boulders extend along the east side of the lake, making hiking difficult by the time the lake comes into view. To get to the south end of the lake, walk down the ridge about 200 yards (183 m) before gradually turning west to the lake. To get to the north end of the lake, stay high on the ridge before eventually dropping down to the very north end. By remaining high on the ridge, hikers avoid some of the large boulders along the lake. The trail on the west side of the lake is the best way to walk from the north end to the south end, but you'll have to climb two large rocky ridges.

As mentioned earlier, an old mule trail from perhaps 80 years ago has disappeared. This trail led along the ridge east of Green Lake and around to the south end. Google Maps shows a thin line in the trees east and south of the lake where the old trail is located. The trail eventually crossed the outlet stream from the lake 0.5 mile (0.8 km) down the hill leading to the Rock Creek Trail from Brownes Lake to Waukena Lake. In years past, that may have been a good approach to Green Lake and may still be a good approach if the USDA Forest Service revives the trail and maintains it.

Most of my 18 trips to the three lakes have been from the trailhead on Cherry Creek. In early or mid-June, snowshoes should be carried for the first half of the hike and used for the snow at higher elevations. Deep snow covers logs and rocks, smoothing the way. Do not expect good fishing until ice is off the lakes after June 20.

Old trails exist along the ridge east of Granite Lake above Trapper Creek. Two miles (3.2 km) east of the Hecla Mine buildings (45°37'03"N

112°53'05"W), a four-wheeler trail begins and continues up the ridge two miles gaining 1,000 feet (305 m) in elevation. Game trails lead to the bottom of an open hillside. At the top of the open hillside (45°35'40"N 112°53'36"W), a trail connects to the north end of the long meadow east of Granite Lake. This approach requires a four-mile (6.4 km) trek with a 1,600-foot (488 m) climb to Granite Lake. Elk hunters with horses frequent this area.

I have reached the lakes by climbing the ridge above Trapper Creek, and I have found that any approach will be a challenge. Just east of the Hecla Mine buildings, an old prospector's trail leads through the timber to a steep shale slope; refer to Google Maps for details. From the top of the slope, continue up and around the hill to find the trail toward Granite Lake. The total hike to Granite Lake is two miles (3.2 km) with a 1,200-foot (366 m) elevation gain; 400 feet (122 m) of that elevation increase is on steep terrain.

I found the Rockvine Penstemon on the steep shale slope in late July. The Rockvine Penstemon is the beautiful twin sister to the Shrubby Penstemon. Refer to the discussion of Grouse Lakes in Chapter 4. The beautiful flowers are quite similar, but the leaves are different.

Another approach to Granite Lake is to climb up the very steep avalanche chute a mile west of the mine buildings. Other people use this approach, and it is similar to the route up the shale slope. I have climbed near the avalanche chute several times, but I prefer climbing the steep shale slope.

The last time that I climbed the ridge near the avalanche chute, I sat down to eat my lunch near the timberline at the top of the hill. All around me, thousands of Snowlover Penstemons and several hundred pink Pygmy Bitterroot flowers bloomed. Near my feet, there was a large bunch of white Mountain Heather. A bunch of brilliant pink Mountain Heather and green or yellow Mountain Heather bloomed nearby. The pink Mountain Heather can be abundant in wet areas above the timberline, but the other flowers are usually uncommon.

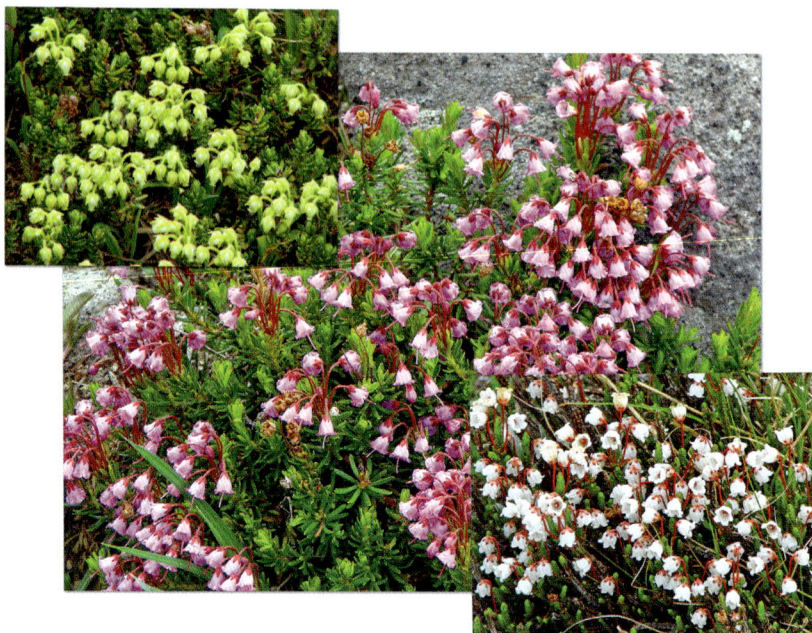

Mountain Heather, July 27, 2010

Sitting in the middle of thousands of Snowlover Penstemons and numerous pink Pygmy Bitterroot flowers was a rare occasion. Several different wildflowers can be found in the marshy ground in the upper Trapper Creek drainage and on the steep slope leading to Granite Lake. For those who like wildflowers and a challenging hike, this would be a good climb.

ENTERING AT THE GLEN EXIT

Brownes, Agnes, Rainbow, and Waukena Lakes are in this area.

BROWNES LAKE

Brownes Lake is a large lake and a good lake for camping and canoeing families. The lake's elevation of 6,560 feet (2,000 m) means

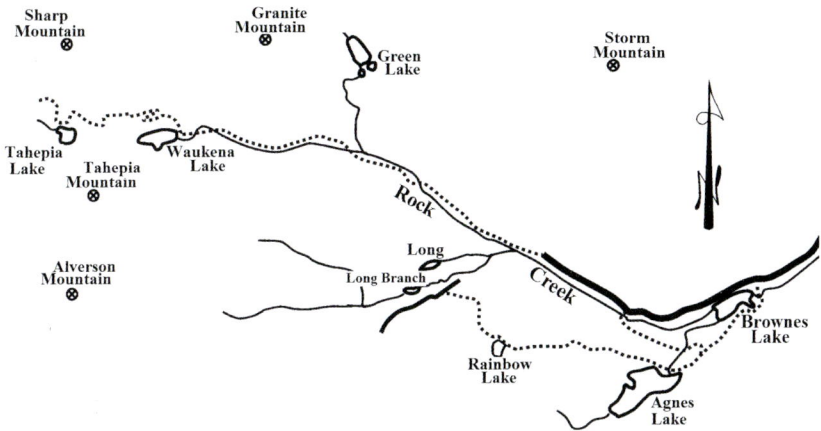

that it may be free of ice by mid-May. The fishing is poor to medium for mostly small fish, but the advantage of this lake is that a good road leads up to it from Interstate 15. Some people fish Rock Creek, which flows into the lake. This lake used to be an improved lake with a small

Brownes Lake looking north from the trail to Agnes Lake. Notice the road on the north side and the faint waterline for the water level before the dam washed out. June 23, 2009.

dam at the outlet, but this small dam washed out June 20, 1984. As a result, the lake water level lowered by eight feet (2.4 m).

The road to Brownes Lake begins at the Glen exit, eight miles (13 km) south of Melrose on Interstate 15. After leaving Interstate 15, drive north along the frontage road for 0.5 mile (0.8 km) before turning west on Rock Creek Road for seven miles (11 km). The dirt road is good to Brownes Lake, but the road around the north side of the lake is one-way on an open, rocky slope. This portion of the road is a little scary the first time. If you're hauling horses, bring a trailer with a narrow wheelbase, and send a partner ahead to clear the way of possible oncoming traffic at the other end of the lake before starting out.

AGNES LAKE

Agnes Lake is the largest lake in the Pioneer Mountains with a surface area of 109 acres (44 hectares). This is a good lake to take children to catch their first fish since it is filled with beautiful arctic grayling that fight to jump on a hook. The fish spawn in mid-June and are easy to catch early in the season. By August, grayling become inactive. The east end of the lake is shallow and easily waded. A few campsites are nearby. The hike to this lake is also a good trip to make on snowshoes in early May.

There are two approaches to Agnes Lake. For most of the summer, begin from the east end of Brownes Lake. Cross the stream on a bridge and climb for a steep 1.6 miles (2.6 km), gaining 1,000 feet (305 m). A second approach, best after spring runoff, is to drive one mile (1.6 km) past Brownes Lake to the stream. The old bridge has been removed, so wade the stream, which is dangerous during high water in June. Later in the summer, the stream can be jumped. This easier approach requires a 1.5-mile (2.4 km) hike with an 800-foot (244 m) elevation gain.

The same trail also leads to Rainbow Lake 2.5 miles (4.0 km) hike past Agnes Lake.

WAUKENA LAKE

Waukena Lake (45°33'08"N 112°57'05"W) is large, exceptionally beautiful, and productive. This lake has a small dam at the outlet. The hike to the lake is well worth the trip.

One year I watched 30 elk graze on the high ridge south of the lake, and another year I saw several mountain goats rest on the peaks north of the lake. Several drainages south between Waukena and Tendoy Lakes provide elk habitat, while the rugged ridges north of Waukena Lake provide a home for mountain goats. Peaks north of Waukena Lake include Granite and Sharp Mountains, and they may be climbed from Granite Lake, Waukena Lake, or from the very west end of the Trapper Creek drainage.

The trailhead to Waukena Lake is three miles (4.8 km) past Brownes Lake or 10 miles (16 km) from the Interstate 15 exit at Glen. From the trailhead, a five-mile (8.0 km) hike with an elevation gain of 1,700 feet (518 m) accesses Waukena Lake. Most of the trail has been reconstructed, providing a better grade than in the past.

Waukena Lake looking west with Tahepia Mountain in the background. Considerable snow remained on the mountain with some ice on the lake. July 2, 2008.

Waukena Lake can also be reached from Mono Campground, 18 miles (29 km) south of the town of Wise River. Some horse traffic travels from Mono Campground past Tahepia Lake over the ridge to Waukena Lake and eventually to Brownes Lake. The distance is 17 miles (27 km) from Mono Campground to Brownes Lake.

APEX JUNCTION

Apex Junction is 10 miles (16 km) north of Dillon and 20 miles (32 km) south of Melrose on Interstate 15. A good dirt road from Apex follows Birch Creek for several miles and branches in several directions. Numerous lakes and several camping areas dot this route. At 10 miles (16 km), the north road leads over the hill to lakes north of Torrey Mountain, and the west branch leads to lakes east and south of Torrey Mountain. All together, 28 lakes are in this region, and some of those lakes are exceptionally nice.

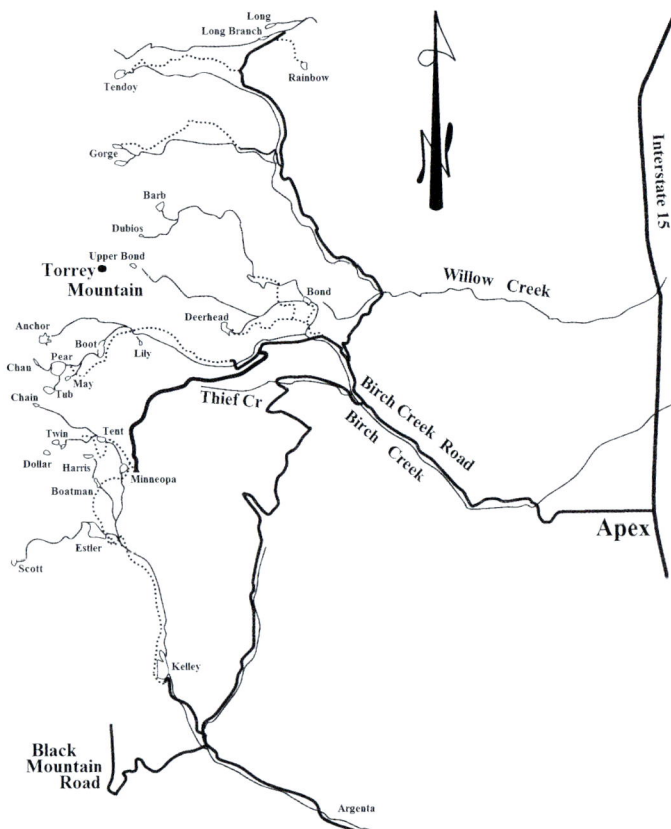

The lakes at the very north end of the road will be discussed first, with the lakes south of Torrey and Tent Mountain considered last.

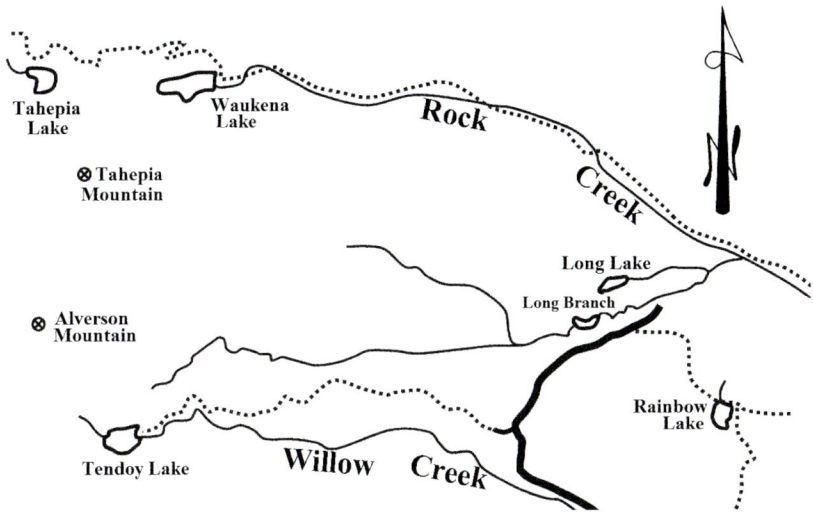

RAINBOW LAKE

Rainbow Lake (45°31'12"N 112°52'36"W) is a small lake with some good fishing, but since the lake is small and easily accessible, the fishing is usually poor. Years ago, when fewer people visited the lake, the fish had a chance to grow larger.

The trailhead (45°31'42"N 112°53'23"W) to the lake is at the very northern end of 20 miles (32 km) of good dirt road from Apex, but slower travel and a high-clearance vehicle would be helpful for the last five miles (8.0 km). The hike requires a one-mile (1.6 km) walk around the ridge with a small elevation gain. An alternate approach to the lake is a 2.5-mile (4.0 km) hike with an elevation change of 400 feet (122 m) from Agnes Lake. A third approach is the uphill trail from Willow Creek. The trailhead for the uphill trail is often used for overnight camping or for horse-trailer parking.

LONG LAKE AND LONG BRANCH LAKE

Long Lake and Long Branch Lake are actually two large ponds near the end of Birch Creek Road. Water seeps into Long Lake at most

Long Branch Lake with the mountains surrounding Tendoy Lake in the background, a peaceful campsite. July 18, 2009.

points around the lake, and water seeps out through a floating mat of grass and roots. Long Branch Lake is a slightly larger lake with considerably more water flowing through it, and features a camping area nearby. This lake holds a few eastern brook trout. Elk and moose frequent the area during the summer and early fall. Long Branch Lake is 0.25 mile (0.4 km) from the road. Long Lake is in the timber 0.5 mile (0.8 km) around the east end of Long Branch Lake. Campers willing to negotiate the trees, big rocks, and mud holes can drive down to Long Branch Lake; of course, a four-wheel-drive vehicle and some daring is needed.

TENDOY LAKE

Tendoy Lake (45°31'05"N 112°57'45"W), at timberline, sits at an elevation of 9,250 feet (2,819 m), and it is one of the most beautiful lakes in the Pioneer Mountains. This lake is the deepest lake in the Pioneers at 100 feet (30 m) deep with a large flow of water. Fishing can be poor since the lake is deep and cold, and because it is easily accessed by four-wheelers. A self-imposed limit of two fish would be appropriate. This is a good lake to snowshoe into in early June or for a winter visit aboard a snowmobile.

Climbing the open grassy slope above the lake to the south is good exercise. An abundance of wildflowers bloom in July. Small birds nest in the sparse cover, and often, fresh goat tracks appear in the snow while tufts of white hair snag on shrubs, indicating that the goats hide nearby. Set aside an hour to climb the 900 foot (274 m) from the lake to the ridgetop, which offers vistas south across an open drainage toward Gorge Lakes with Tweedy and Torrey Mountains in the background. A little more walking leads to a view down into the David Creek drainage to the west.

On one of my trips to Tendoy Lake, I caught my two-fish limit, and one of the cutthrout trout was shaped like a slab-sided bluegill.

The trailhead is located on a good dirt road 18 miles (29 km) west and north of Apex on Interstate 15. Turn left from the main dirt road for 100 yards (91 m) to the trailhead at 45°31'06"N 112°54'31"W.

Tendoy Lake in early July with the remains of winter evident. David Creek, which leads to Torrey Lake, is over the mountain to the west. July 9, 2008.

The lake is an easy 3.2-mile (5.1 km) hike with an elevation gain of 1,200 feet (366 m). Motorized use is not allowed beyond the first 1.5 mile of trail.

Chief Tendoy, a Lemhi Shoshone Indian, died in May 1907 and was buried near Tendoy, Idaho. The Tendoy Mountains are a small range of mountains west of Interstate 15 between Clark Canyon Reservoir and Lima, at the southern end of the Beaverhead Mountain Range.

THE TRAILHEAD TO GORGE LAKES

The trailhead to Gorge Lakes (45°29'38"N 112°54'29"W) is located 18 miles (29 km) from Apex and Interstate 15.

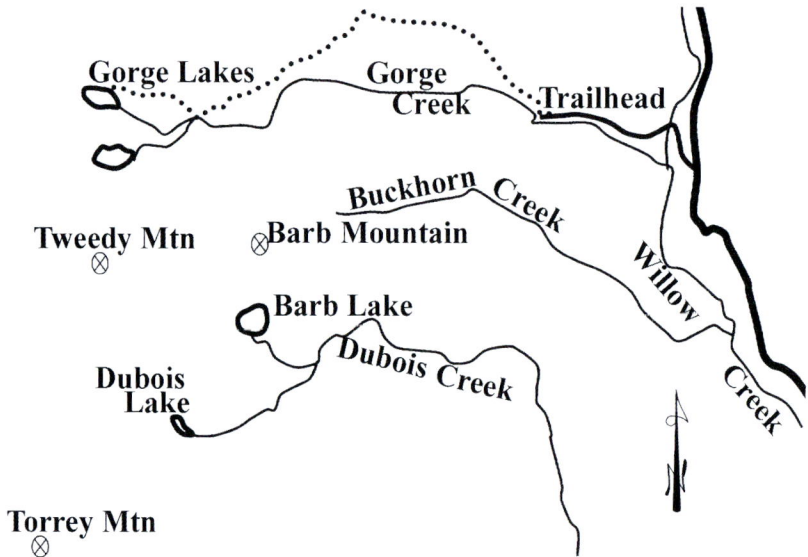

GORGE LAKE NORTH AND GORGE LAKE SOUTH

Gorge Lake North (45°29'41"N 112°57'51"W) and Gorge Lake South are also among the most beautiful lakes in the Pioneer Mountains. An artist would appreciate these two lakes. Both lakes feature distinctive rocks on their south sides. These rocks may be climbed without technical gear, but technical rock climbers would also appreciate the rocks and some rocks on the west side of Tweedy Mountain. Tweedy Mountain can be climbed beginning from South Gorge Lake up a very steep avalanche chute, but climbing the peak beginning from Barb Lake on the south side of the mountain (Barb Mountain) is a better route and has the same elevation gain of 2,000 feet (610 m) as from South Gorge Lake.

Snowshoeing into the lakes in early June is good exercise. Leave the fishing pole at home and take the camera. With ice and snow covering the lakes and mountains, the small avalanches and falling rocks are more frequent and sound louder than later in the summer. During early spring, bears wander around, perhaps looking for the black or dark green moss that drops from the trees during the winter. One spring, I found a large bear track in the snow with a very small track that followed. I had just missed those two ursine inhabitants, and later in the afternoon when I returned, the snow had melted, and the tracks had disappeared. On another occasion, a friend and I hiked into North Gorge Lake on October 19. The snow was deep, with a cold wind sweeping across the lake, but the fishing was quite good. My friend was afraid of bears; therefore, I did not tell him of the fresh mountain lion tracks on the trail.

Encountering fresh tracks of the big cat is exciting at any time, since the felines are secretive and elusive. Often the footprint of the back foot will be in the same spot as the front print with a 30-inch (76 cm) stride. Rarely will a person have a chance to see a mountain lion, but the big cats usually hide near wherever the deer are in early spring. On one occasion, I was climbing a steep rock, but I backed off because of the danger and since I was alone. When I climbed up around the rock to the top by an easier route, I found a fresh mountain lion footprint in the wet sand.

These lakes are usually (but not always) good producers of 12- to 18-inch (30 to 46 cm) trout. Good fly-fishing is possible at either lake, but the west end of Gorge Lake South can be especially good. Ice may remain on the lakes into the first week of July, since both lakes occur near 9,200 feet (2,804 m) in elevation. I have been disappointed after hiking for three hours to find the north lake still frozen on July 6, but on another occasion the lakes were ice free on June 28.

The Gorge Lakes trailhead (45°29'38"N 112°54'29"W) is located 18 miles (29 km) from Apex and Interstate 15. Most of the road is a good dirt road except for the last three miles (4.8 km) after it branches from the main road. Slower driving is required for this portion of the road, and a high-clearance vehicle would be helpful. For a couple of summers, a very large rock nearly blocked this side road. The trail to

Sunset at North Gorge Lake. The ridge in view is the east end of Barb Mountain. Notice that the north-facing ridges are barren of vegetation at higher elevations. August 4, 2011.

South Gorge Lake looking east toward Barb Mountain. The steep avalanche chute leading up to Tweedy Mountain begins at the west end of this lake from near where the picture was taken. July 28, 2006.

North Gorge Lake requires a four-mile (6.4 km) hike with an elevation gain of 1,650 feet (503 m) on a good horse trail. The trail to South Gorge Lake includes a 0.5-mile (0.8 km) section on a steep, rocky ridge to the south on an indistinct trail; no horse trail exists on the steep, rocky slope. When leaving South Gorge Lake, it is best to drop over the hill to the small meadow before joining the trail again at a lower elevation. An overgrown trail from the meadow to South Gorge Lake existed at one time, and horses could get to the lake by that approach. Of course, the trail is steep, requiring some effort. The trail to both lakes led through the small meadow at one time.

The drainage north of the lakes is well worth extra attention. Turn north off the trail 0.5 mile (0.8 km) before the lakes. Both elk and mountain goats may be in this beautiful drainage. This detour will require an additional hour or more of walking. At the top of the ridge, look west down into the David Creek drainage leading to Torrey Lake, and also south to North Gorge Lake with a good view of both Tweedy

75

and Torrey Mountains. The upper part of that drainage was nearly covered with white Mountain Heather in early August one year.

BARB LAKE

Barb Lake (45°28'33"N 112°56'38"W) is located on the southeast side of Tweedy Mountain and south of Barb Mountain at an elevation of 9,200 feet (2,804 m). These tall peaks can be seen from Interstate 15 north of Dillon. No trail leads to Barb Lake, but the 2.5- to 4-hour hike is well worth the extra effort. The lake is both beautiful and productive for fishing. The lake's surface area of 13 acres (5.3 hectares) deepens to 50 feet (15 m), with a significant flow of water through the lake. This large flow of water probably causes the ice to melt a little earlier than other lakes at a similar elevation. A nice, white sandy beach on the east end accommodates wading and fly-fishing.

This lake is especially nice because the fishing is usually quite good, the lake provides a high-mountain experience with isolation, and the hike to the lake is difficult and challenging. A good path to the lake would make the experience less enjoyable.

I have hiked to Barb Lake eleven times, and all trips were from the Gorge Creek area. On my last trip, I found a large beaver swimming in the lake. He seemed to be lost and probably would not survive the winter. A couple of bald eagles flew above the lake. On one occasion, I arrived at Barb Lake on June 22, finding most of the lake still covered with ice. Little birds hopped around on the edge of the ice. On another occasion, I arrived October 17 to find the ice extending out from the shore for some distance, making it difficult to fish. The Torrey Mountain topographic map, a BLM map, and Google Maps are helpful.

Take Birch Creek Road at Apex, 10 miles (16 km) north of Dillon on Interstate 15, and drive 18 miles (29 km) to the Gorge Creek drainage. In the past, I crossed a wooden bridge near the Gorge Lakes trailhead and drove 1 mile (1.6 km) to the end of the logging road. When I was younger, I immediately climbed the steep brushy slope to the top. Although it was a difficult climb, I enjoyed climbing quickly up the steep slope.

I discovered the large Douglas-fir trees on the north side of Barb Mountain by accident when I came down the ridge west of my truck, near the old wooden bridge. I returned to take pictures and to admire those evergreens on later trips. One of the trees measured 45 inches (1.1 m) in diameter at chest height.

The wooden bridge was removed several years ago, but the same route to Barb Lake remains the best approach once Gorge Creek finishes spring flooding. Park near the creek and follow the old logging road to the end. The serious brush on the north-facing, steep slope of Barb Mountain can be avoided some by climbing the east- and south-facing slopes. Continue around the ridge to the east and south, gaining some elevation. An obscure elk trail follows the steep east-facing ridge to the top. After reaching the top of the ridge, leave some surveyor's tape to relocate the elk trail on the return trip. Continue up the ridge north of Buckhorn Creek or drop down to the small valley and climb the next ridge south to a slight pass. The next drainage south of Buckhorn Creek and this ridge contains Barb Lake and Dubois Creek. That slight pass leading to the Barb Lake drainage is half of the distance and elevation change as the path to Barb Lake.

It is best to remain close to Barb Mountain on the north while climbing the drainage. The steep avalanche chute on the side of Barb Mountain is at the two-thirds point in both distance and elevation from the truck to the lake. This avalanche chute, visible from Interstate 15 north of Dillon, appears white on the Torrey Mountain topographic map. This avalanche chute is discernible on Google Maps too. Avoid climbing too high on the side of Barb Mountain since steep cliffs and rocks block the way.

This first approach to the lake requires a 3.5-mile (5.6 km) hike with an elevation gain of 1,700 feet (518 m). This distance is deceptive, however, because of the climb's difficulty. Expect a hike of three to four hours. When I was younger, I made the climb in 2.5 hours on several occasions.

A second approach begins from near Bond Lake (45°26'17"N 112°52'31"W). Walk one mile (1.6 km) west toward Deerhead Lake on a four-wheeler trail before turning north on another four-wheeler trail for two more miles (3.2 km) to the end of the irrigation ditch to Bond Lake (45°27'10"N 112°54'11"W). The irrigation ditch from Bond Lake may be nearly dry by late summer. The hike from Bond Lake to Barb Lake is seven miles (11 km) with an elevation gain of 2,000 feet (610 m). By using a four-wheeler or a trail bike on the first part of the trail, the hike will be shorter but the elevation change will be about the same. This would be the preferred approach for most folks.

Much more effort is required, but it's also possible to hike or climb from Gorge Lakes to the north. This approach would require a difficult

Barb Lake, August 6, 2010

climb on Tweedy Mountain up the very steep avalanche chute from South Gorge Lake. A few folks have climbed over the steep ridge from Torrey Lake to the west.

A small, beautiful blue-green pond (called Dubois Lake on some maps) nestles one mile (1.6 km) southwest of Barb Lake. From the ridge west of Dubois Lake, you can look down on Torrey and Glacier Lakes farther west.

On the previous page is a view of Barb Lake from near Dubois Lake looking north toward Barb Mountain. Notice the craggy nature of the south-facing slope of Barb Mountain. The north-facing slope viewed from Gorge Lakes to the north is a far more rugged ascent. Tweedy Mountain anchors the western end of the ridge leading to Barb Mountain. The ascent of Tweedy Mountain from Barb Lake would require an additional 2,000-foot (610 m) climb.

THE TRAIL TO BOND AND DEERHEAD LAKES

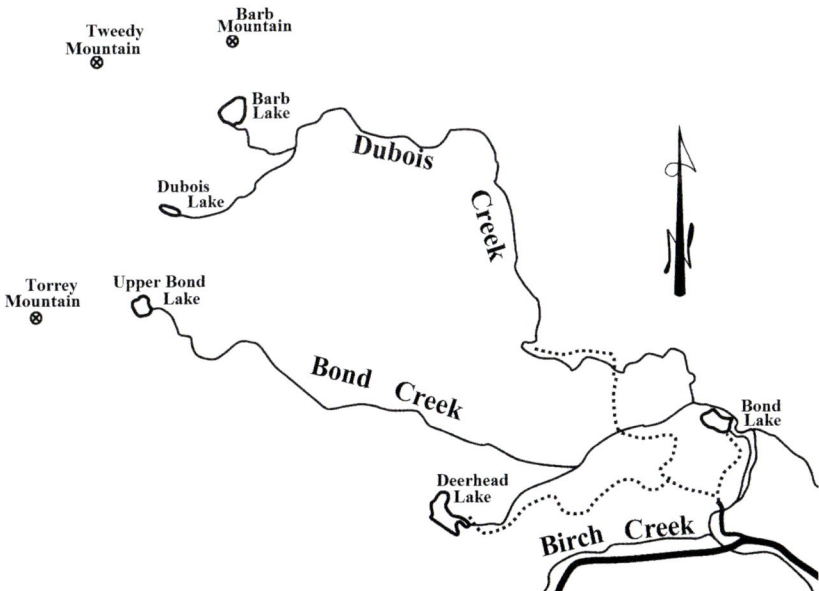

BOND LAKE

Bond Lake is used for irrigation purposes and has few fish. The lake is accessible on a four-wheeler trail one mile (1.6 km) from the trail to Deerhead Lake. The lake fills during spring, but mostly dries by August.

Bond Lake looking west to Torrey Mountain in the background beyond the more prominent, smaller peaks. Forty elk grazed along the west side of the lake when this picture was taken. June 16, 2009.

DEERHEAD LAKE

Deerhead Lake (45°26'13"N 112°54'53"W) is located on the east slope of Torrey Mountain and provides only fair fishing. The lake, at 7,600 feet (2,316 m) elevation, is at the end of a good four-wheeler trail. A three-mile (4.8 km) hike with a 600-foot (183 m) elevation gain begins near Bond Lake. Another approach is the climb from Dinner Station

Deerhead Lake, June 16, 2009

Campground with an elevation gain of 400 feet (122 m). The trail to Deerhead Lake branches south from the more prominent trail to the drainage ditch to Lower Bond Lake after a one-mile (1.6 km) hike. A good four-wheel-drive truck can travel part way. I have driven part of the four-wheeler trail in the past. The road continues to deteriorate, making the drive quite difficult except for four-wheelers. Some emergency road repairs such as removing rocks and clearing downed trees may be necessary.

On one trip, I found an aluminum boat stashed in the grass on the west side of the lake. The boat was in poor condition since some thoughtless person had shot a few holes in it.

Above is a view of Deerhead Lake. The east end of the ridge leading to Torrey Mountain appears near the photo's center. The other peak is east of Torrey Mountain and south of Barb Lake. Upper Bond Lake is in the upper valley between the two distant peaks in this view.

A Torrey Mountain climb could begin from Deerhead Lake, but this climb requires an additional 3,600-foot (1,097 m) elevation gain. The total elevation gain from the Dinner Station Campground would be slightly more than 4,000 feet (1,219 m), challenging for any athlete. A better approach may be to climb from Upper Bond Lake.

UPPER BOND LAKE

Upper Bond Lake (45°27'25"N 112°57'31"W) is a large, beautiful pond at 9,300 feet (2,835 m) in the large bowl east of Torrey Mountain. Although water flows during summer, the flow may diminish during the winter, as the lake freezes nearly to the bottom. This lake has no campfire rings and is challenging to access, yet it remains a good starting point to climb Torrey Mountain.

To access this large pond and drainage, climb the ridge north of and overlooking Deerhead Lake. At some point on the ridge, drop down slightly, following a steep elk trail into the drainage leading to the pond. Move to the drainage midsection to avoid rock fields next to the ridge. Move into the drainage north of the ridge at anypoint from just above Deerhead Lake to 1.5 miles (2.4 km) up the ridge. I find that when traveling to Upper Bond Lake, I move north into that drainage from just above Deerhead Lake and, when returning, I climb the ridge as soon the rocky slopes allow.

The three-mile (4.8 km) climb from Deerhead Lake to Upper Bond Lake requires an elevation gain of 1,700 feet (518 m). From near Bond Lake, the hike would be six miles (9.7 km) with an elevation gain of 2,300 feet (701 m).

Many small trees surrounding Upper Bond Lake are stunted by the harsh winter winds. On my last trip I found a western toad near the lake as it posed for its picture. That toad had probably hibernated most of its life, and it may be old. I can imagine that little spot in the gravel has been her castle for several cold summers and much colder winters. A mile (1.6 km) below the lake, I found the flower Pink Spiraea.

The outlet stream from Upper Bond Lake looking west to Torrey Mountain. August 12, 2010. A Western toad and the wildflower Pink Spiraea.

On another occasion to Upper Bond Lake, a small squirrel hid in the motor area of my truck. I supposed that it would leave when I started the engine, but after driving for one hour, including part of it at interstate speeds, I noticed a small squirrel tail sticking out from under the hood. By the time that I was able to stop and open the hood the frightened little hitchhiker was gone. I wished him the very best.

Upper Bond Lake is suitable for camping and then continuing the climb of Torrey Mountain. A long, steep, grassy slope just south of the lake begins the nearly 2,000-foot (610 m) elevation gain. The ridge just north of the lake can be climbed from the lake. Few people will ever venture on the ridge north of Upper Bond Lake, which is the same steep rocky ridge that is south from Barb Lake.

LAKES WEST FROM THE DINNER STATION CAMPGROUND

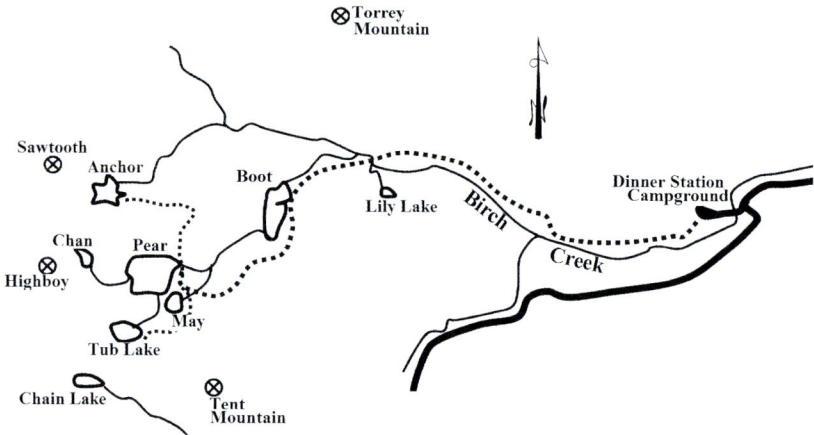

LILY, BOOT, PEAR, MAY, TUB, CHAN, AND ANCHOR LAKES

Seven lakes in the same general proximity, all south and west of Torrey Mountain, lack good fishing except Tub Lake. Tub, Chan, and Anchor Lakes have open, rocky slopes on one side. Tub and Anchor Lakes are at almost 9,200 feet (2,804 m) and often remain iced in through the 4th of July. Most of these lakes have small dams, which drain during the July and August irrigation season. Most of the water is drained for irrigation from Boot, Pear, and Anchor Lakes as well, resulting in poor fishing. I found a broken arrowhead at May Lake on one of my visits. I would like to know its story. I imagine that after being hit with an arrow, a moose escaped to the mountains and died many years later of old age.

The trailhead (45°25'40"N 112°54'23"W) is 0.5 mile (0.8 km) from the Dinner Station Campground,12 miles (19.3 km) west of Interstate 15 at Apex. A deteriorated road leads from the campground to Pear Lake. A high-clearance truck could travel all of the way if necessary, but a better approach is to drive part way and then hike the remaining distance. A four-wheeler can get to Pear Lake easily, and a motor bike can access the remaining lakes. The exception is Chan Lake, which has no trail. Chan Lake is mostly filled by a centuries-old rock glacier east of 10,431-foot (3,179 m) Highboy Mountain. Google Maps and Google Earth reveal this interesting geological feature which is easily mistaken for a rock fall or slide. In contrast to sudden rock falls, a rock glacier forms over centuries. Those in the southeastern Pioneers appear to be inactive, formed in an era when the region received considerably more snow. The resulting glaciers grinding against the mountains accumulated layers of talus rock. The foot of such a rock glacier often holds a small lake, such as Chan Lake and West Twin Lake.

The distance from the Dinner Station Campground to Tub and Anchor Lakes is 6.5 miles (10 km) with a 2,000-foot (610 m) elevation gain.

LILY LAKE

Lily Lake of the East Pioneer Mountains is a shallow lily pond just south of where the trail to Pear Lake crosses Birch Creek. (Lily Lake of the West Pioneer Mountains is a much larger lake and has good fishing.) Boot Lake is a mile (1.6 km) beyond Lily Lake and the stream crossing.

CHAIN LAKE

Chain Lake or pond is located at 9,700 feet (2,957 m) at the top of the steep rocky slope above Tub Lake. A climb up a steep avalanche chute for an additional 600-foot (183 m) elevation gain is necessary. The advantage of this climb is that a magnificent panoramic view of all the lakes in the valley below joins a view of Torrey Mountain to the northeast. Mountain goats frequent this area. Chain Lake can be reached most easily from Minneopa and Tent Lakes to the south of Tent Mountain.

The pass just east of Tent Mountain is a good spot to photograph the lakes. This pass can also be used to get to the lakes from the south. I used that approach one time in the past, but it requires a significant increase and decrease in elevation and crossing a large avalanche rock field. A distance of 2.5 miles (4.0 km) with an elevation increase and decrease of 1,800 feet (549 m) is required to reach May Lake.

Below is a photograph from the pass just east of Tent Mountain. Near the bottom of the picture is the rock field and avalanche area. May Lake is just south of the more visible Pear Lake. Tub Lake is hidden behind the north slope of Tent Mountain. Chan Lake is just east of Highboy Mountain in the middle of the picture. Anchor Lake is on the timbered ridge north of Pear Lake. The south end of Sawtooth Mountain is just above Pear Lake and Anchor Lake.

Pear Lake, September 24, 2008

Looking north from the pass just east of Tent Mountain, the view features Torrey Mountain with Boot Lake below. September 24, 2008.

THE TRAILHEAD TO LAKES SOUTH OF TENT MOUNTAIN

The trailhead to lakes south of Tent Mountain is 17 miles (27 km) from Apex on Interstate 15. Drive past the turnoff road to Dinner Station Campground for an additional five miles (8 km).

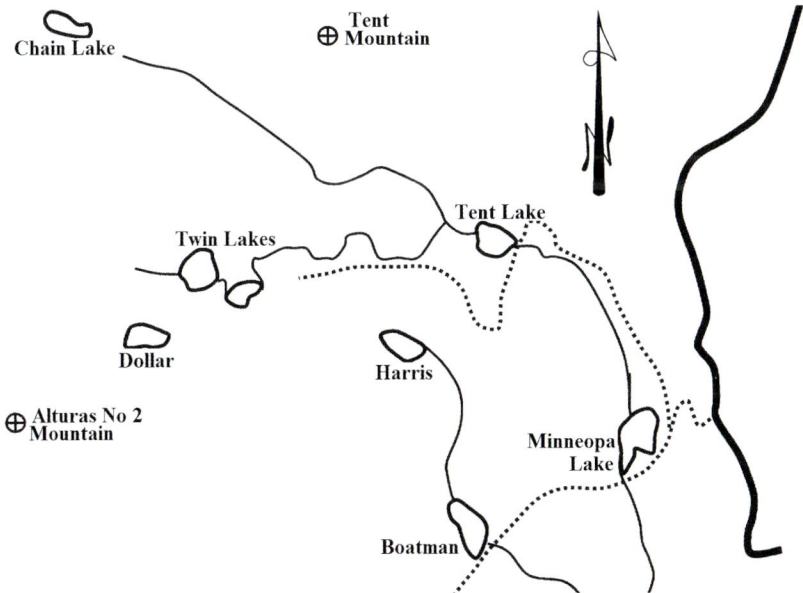

MINNEOPA LAKE

Minneopa Lake was dammed with the water level about 10 feet (3 m) deeper than it is now. Since the dam washed out, the water level has dropped, leaving a large, shallow pond with few fish. Fly fishermen with float tubes enjoy this lake thanks to a few fish, normally gentle winds, and warm water. Occasionally, a bald eagle flies around the area seeking the fish or ducks in the shallow water.

The trailhead (45°23'41"N 112°57'30"W) to Minneopa Lake is at the end of the Birch Creek Road 17 miles (27 km) from Apex on Interstate 15. The lake is a 0.25-mile (0.4 km) walk from the trailhead. This lake is the starting point for hikes to several other lakes in the area. These lakes include Tent, Harris, Dollar, Chain, and Twin Lakes to the north, and Boatman, Estler, and Scott Lakes to the south.

Minneopa Lake with Tent Mountain in the background to the north. The shallow lake provides a lovely reflective surface most mornings. July 7, 2007.

TENT LAKE

Tent Lake is one mile (1.6 km) around the northern end of Minneopa Lake on a good horse trail. Tent Lake was dammed, but the dam washed out, leaving a shallow pond with few fish.

HARRIS LAKE

Harris Lake (45°23'50"N 112°58'50"W) was improved but the dam washed out here too. This lake is a one-mile (1.6 km) walk with an elevation gain of 300 feet (91 m) from Tent Lake. Even though a good horse trail leads from Tent Lake to Twin Lakes, the best approach is a walk through the timber to Harris Lake and then toward Twin Lakes or to Dollar Lake. Numerous water critters paddle and splash here, but no fish exist in Harris Lake. The first time that I hiked to Harris Lake was from Boatman Lake to the south.

Harris Lake with Alturas No. 2 Mountain in the background to the west. Dollar Lake is just north of the mountain peak near the middle of the picture, and Twin Lakes are east of the ridge at the right side of the picture. September 19, 2008.

DOLLAR LAKE

Dollar Lake (45°23'53"N 113°00'00"W), near the top of the 9,200-foot (2,804 m) ridge, hangs in a beautiful alpine setting, north and east of Alturas No. 2 Mountain. No visible inlet or outlet feeds this lake; however, a few small springs in the bottom of the lake resupply some water. From Minneopa Lake, Dollar Lake is a three-mile (4.8 km) walk with an elevation gain of 1,000 feet (305 m). Walk past Tent and Harris Lakes keeping near the ridge to the south. Dollar Lake sits above, up a steep, rocky ridge beyond Twin Lakes. Alturas No. 2 Mountain can be climbed from Dollar Lake with a 1,300-foot (396 m) elevation gain. Below is a view of Dollar Lake with Alturas No. 2 Mountain in the background. The lake is deeper in June and July.

Dollar Lake with Alturas No. 2 Mountain, August 26, 2013

TWIN LAKES

The main Twin Lake near the rocky ridge usually has the best fishing because of its considerable size and depth. This larger Twin Lake is the only lake in this area with fishing, since Tent and Minneopa have just a few fish. Still, the fishing is only moderate, but the lake is scenic and especially beautiful during September's fall foliage, when red shrubbery lines the shore. Small springs enter the lake at several places around the perimeter. Those springs appear to seep from the large rock glacier that filled the west part of the lake centuries ago. At that time, the lake would may been larger and the mountain would have been taller.

A horse trail crosses the stream at Tent Lake and winds around to Twin Lakes. The trail used to be hard to find, but with more folks visiting Twin Lakes, the trail is now quite easy to follow. When by myself, I usually cut through the timber, departing from the trail.

The distance to Twin Lakes from Minneopa Lake is three miles (4.8 km) with a 700-foot (213 m) elevation gain.

Below is a view of the second or West Twin Lake. Notice the results of the large rock glacier just west of the lake. Dollar Lake is up over the rocky ridge to the south.

West Twin Lake, August 30, 2011

CHAIN LAKE

Chain Lake (45°24'48"N 113°00'21"W) is really a medium-sized pond at an elevation of 9,700 feet (2,957 m), the highest-elevation lake in the Pioneer Mountains. This shallow lake above timberline probably freezes solid during winter. Snow usually banks up along the west side of the lake and hangs over the ridgetop even into August and September. The advantage of this location is the magnificent panoramic view of all of the lakes in the valley just west of Torrey Mountain: Boot, Pear, May, Tub, and Anchor Lakes as well as Torrey Mountain fill in the background.

Highboy Mountain can be reached from Chain Lake with a 700-foot (213 m) elevation gain. Mountain goats frequent the area. My idea of a good goat hunt would be to climb the ridge between Alturas No. 2 and Highboy Mountains with a pair of binoculars. Goats sport their long winter coats after mid-November.

Chain Lake can be reached by a 600-foot (183 m) climb up a steep, rocky ridge from Tub Lake north of Tent Mountain, or by walking

Torrey Mountain from near Chain Lake, September 30, 2006

past Minneopa, Tent, and Twin Lakes from south of Tent Mountain. Travel north from Twin Lakes over the small ridge through an alpine basin to another small but steep sandy ridge to Chain Lake. With care, horses could probably reach the alpine basin below the lake. From Minneopa Lake, the four-mile (6.4 km) route climbs 1,600 feet (488 m). When leaving Chain Lake, hikers can follow the drainage down to Tent Lake or retrace the hike past Twin Lakes for a gentler descent. The beautiful scenery surrounding Chain Lake is well worth the effort.

The previous page provides a view of Torrey Mountain from near Chain Lake. This picture was taken looking northeast with Pear Lake in the middle of the picture. Tub Lake is at the bottom of the picture with May Lake slightly south of Pear Lake. Boot Lake is in the distance at the edge of the picture. The picture also shows the long drainage west and south of Torrey Mountain; this is one branch of upper Birch Creek. There are several small ponds at the very upper end of that drainage.

TRAIL FROM MINNEOPA LAKE TO BOATMAN, ESTLER, AND SCOTT LAKES

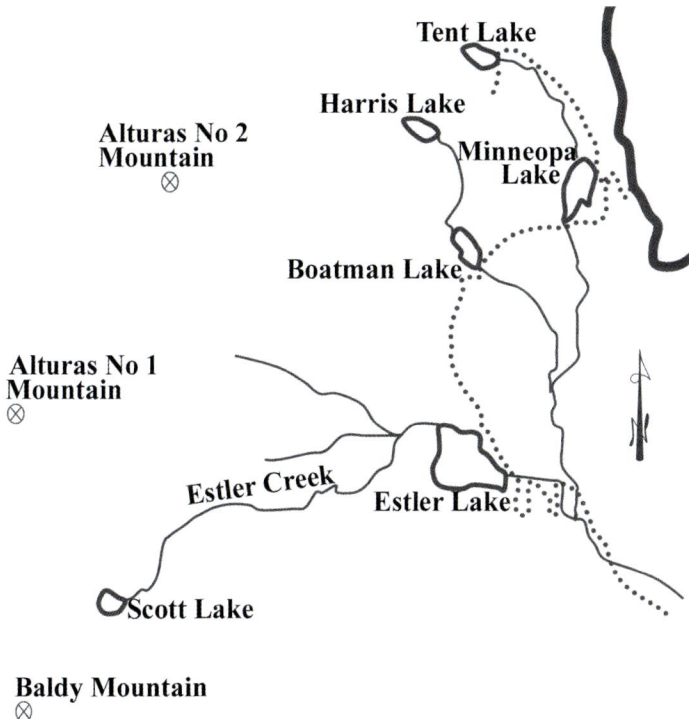

BOATMAN LAKE

Boatman Lake's small dam washed out sometime in the past, leaving a large pond with few fish. This lake is one mile (1.6 km) west of the south end of Minneopa Lake. The photograph of Boatman Lake has Tent Mountain in the background to the north. Harris Lake is a one-mile (1.6 km) climb up the hill north toward Tent Mountain. At one time, some mining occurred just west of the lake, and presently remnants of a large log cabin remain near the lake.

Boatman Lake, September 24, 2008

ESTLER LAKE

Estler Lake is drawn down for irrigation in July and August. As a result, the fishing is poor, but the inlet stream draws a few fish.

The lake is 2.5 miles (4.0 km) past Boatman Lake on the same trail with a 300-foot (91 m) elevation loss from Minneopa Lake. A four-wheeler trail leads from Kelley Reservoir to Estler Lake, five miles (8.0 km) with an elevation gain of 900 feet (274 m).

Estler Lake looking west with Baldy Mountain in the background. Scott Lake is east of the tallest peak of Baldy Mountain and north of the patch of timber on the mountainside. September 24, 2008.

SCOTT LAKE

Scott Lake (45°21'49"N 113°01'00"W) is an exceptionally beautiful lake just east of Baldy Mountain at 8,700 feet (2,652 m). Alturas No. 1 and No. 2 peaks rise to the north of Scott Lake with Polaris Lake over the pass to the west and between the two peaks. A high, steep ridge connects Baldy Mountain with Alturas No. 1 and No. 2, providing a home for mountain goats. On one of my visits, several mountain goats appeared high on the mountain above Scott Lake.

Scott Lake occasionally provides good fishing for the few people who find the lake. The lake is small with moderate depth, and flowing water for the entire year. Estler Creek from Scott Lake to Estler Lake often harbors a few nice fish during summer. The Estler Creek area shelters elk during the summer and early elk-hunting season each fall. Snowmobilers apparently visit Scott Lake in winter.

Finding the lake could be a challenge. Beginning on the north side of Estler Lake, hike through the timber; there is no trail. Remain on the ridge just south or near Estler Creek for 1.5 miles (2.4 km), gaining 900 feet (274 m). When returning from Scott Lake, remain close to Estler Creek for the entire distance.

Scott Lake with Baldy Mountain in the background to the west, 1,900 feet (580 m) higher in elevation. June 30, 2009.

KELLEY RESERVOIR

Kelley Reservoir is used for irrigation and is nearly drained dry during July and August, requiring most of the fish to migrate into the stream. A rough road wraps around the west side of the lake to the stream and to a small charcoal oven. This reservoir is located just north of Argenta, 20 miles (32 km) northwest of Dillon.

Kelley Reservoir near the outlet looking north toward Estler Lake. June 26, 2009.

Chapter 3

*

ENTERING THE EAST PIONEER MOUNTAINS FROM THE SCENIC BYWAY SOUTH OF WISE RIVER

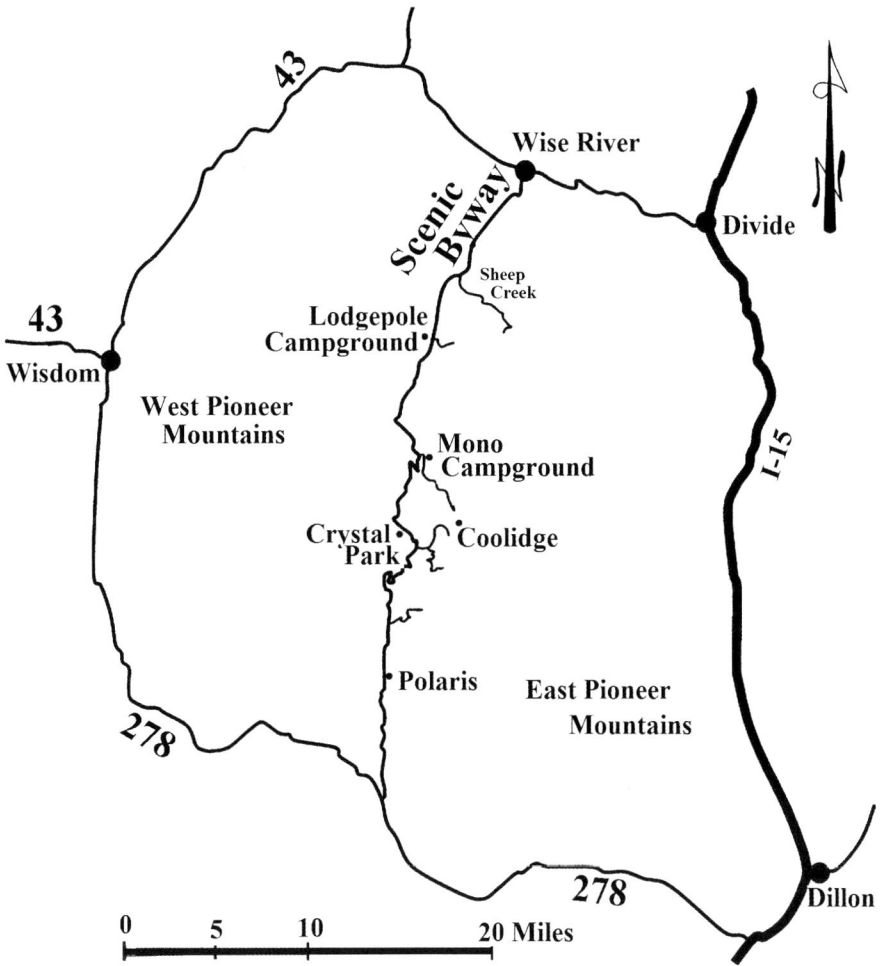

Fourteen lakes in the East Pioneer Mountains can be reached from the paved Pioneer Mountains National Scenic Byway that leads south from the town of Wise River. These lakes include: Bobs, Black Lion, Teacup, Tahepia, Schultz, Torrey, Glacier, Elkhorn, Hall, Hopkins, Dingley, Sawtooth, and Polaris Lakes.

The shortest trail to Bobs Lake begins at the west end of Vipond Park. The approximate coordinates for the trailhead are 45°39'01"N 112°56'55"W.

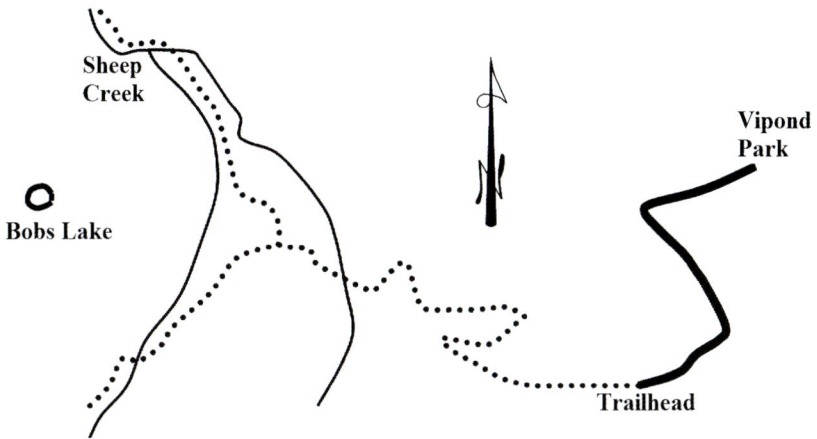

BOBS LAKE

Bobs Lake, (45°39'43"N 112°59'48"W) a small, seldom fished lake, sits at 8,600 feet (2,621 m) near the head of Sheep Creek, three miles (4.8 km) north of Black Lion Mountain (north peak). Small springs on the west side of the lake provide fresh water for the few small fish. The water leaves the lake by seeping into the ground rather than draining through a definite outlet. The Upper Sheep Creek area is favored by elk, which spook when hikers climb to Bobs Lake. Higher on the mountain, some mountain goats may linger. A small pond, belly deep to elk, in upper Sheep Creek holds a few small trout. Elk often wade into this pond to cool off on hot summer days.

To take the shortest of two routes to the lake, head west from the end of the road from Vipond Park. The trail crosses over the pass between Sheep Mountain and Black Lion Mountain (north peak). The trail then drops down into the Sheep Creek drainage. Follow the trail for another mile (1.6 km) up Sheep Creek until about equal in elevation with Bobs Lake before cutting back north along the ridge. The last mile (1.6 km) of the hike travels north around the ridge. No trail exists here. The lake is on a small bench. Climb the bench just south of a small peak, which is easy to recognize but most visible only at the lake and from higher elevations. Perhaps a GPS unit would be helpful in locating the lake. Coordinates and elevations can be found from topographic maps and Google Earth. This first approach requires 4.5 miles (7.2 km) of walking with an elevation change, both up and down, of 1,700 feet (518 m). The return trip also requires a 600-foot (183 m) climb from the Sheep Creek drainage to the pass south of Sheep Mountain.

The second route to Bobs Lake follows Sheep Creek eight miles (13 km) south of the town of Wise River on a good trail from the Flying Cloud Ranch. Four-wheelers can approach within a mile (1.6 km) of the lake. The hike from Flying Cloud Ranch to Bobs Lake is 6.5 miles (10 km) with an elevation gain of 2,300 feet (701 m).

Bobs Lake and the small peak north of the lake. June 29, 2010.

TRAIL TO BLACK LION LAKE

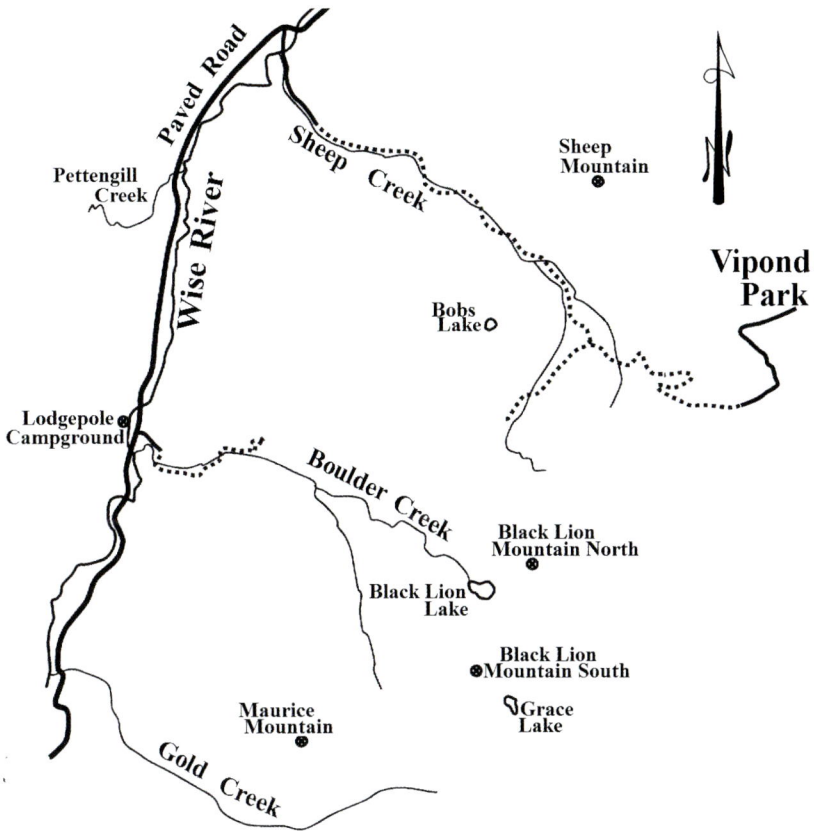

BLACK LION LAKE

Black Lion Lake (45°37'36"N 113° 00'00"W), a deep and beautiful lake at the head of Boulder Creek, rests between Black Lion Mountain North and Black Lion Mountain South at an elevation of 8,800 feet (2,682 m). The lake has the potential for good fishing. A wet fly may be better than a dry fly since the fish tend to remain deep and hard to catch.

Approach this lake by parking at the end of a side road (45°38'51"N 113°04'09"W) on Boulder Creek twelve miles (19 km) south of the town of Wise River. The parking spot is located 0.5 mile (0.8 km) east and across the main paved road from Lodgepole Campground. Follow the trail for one mile (1.6 km) before leaving the trail and continuing up the steep Boulder Creek drainage for a 4.5-mile (7.2 km) climb with an elevation gain of 2,200 feet (671 m), a difficult climb.

If riding four-wheelers, the approach to Black Lion Lake begins at Flying Cloud Ranch. Drive up Sheep Creek 6.5 miles (10 km) to the end of the trail. From the trail's end, hike another three miles (4.8 km) with an elevation gain of 1,000 feet (305 m) to the ridge just north of Black Lion Mountain North and 600 feet (183 m) down and around the ridge. The total hiking distance from Flying Cloud Ranch is nine miles (14 km) with an elevation change, both up and down, of 3,700 feet (1,128 m).

A few folks also hike over the top of Black Lion Mountain from the road's end west of Vipond Park. This approach requires a hike of 5.5

Black Lion Lake appears far below with Black Lion Mountain South and Maurice Mountain in the background. To take this picture, I hiked to the top of Black Lion Mountain from the end of the road west of Vipond Park. July 23, 2010.

miles (8.9 km) with an elevation gain of 1,700 feet (518 m) followed by an elevation loss of 1,300 feet (396 m). At the end of the day, the return trip requires a climb of 1,300 feet (396 m). For those who enjoy hiking more than fishing, the trip provides great panoramic views well above timberline most of the time. This trip should be avoided when lightning storms are likely.

Although I have been to Black Lion Lake only one time, I have been on the mountain above the lake on three other occasions. Years ago, miners exploring for molybdenum disturbed the area, and some of the scars still remain.

On one of my trips to the top of Black Lion Mountain in mid-July, I found a gathering of 300 ladybugs scattered in several rock crevices. July 23, 2010.

MONO CREEK CAMPGROUND

Mono Creek Campground (45°32'06"N 113°04'44"W) is 22 miles (35 km) south of the town of Wise River and is a starting point for travel to several lakes in that drainage. Horses and riders travel on all of the trails, and in the past, four-wheelers and trail bikes were permitted on some trails after midsummer.

When walking, however, another approach includes a drive along

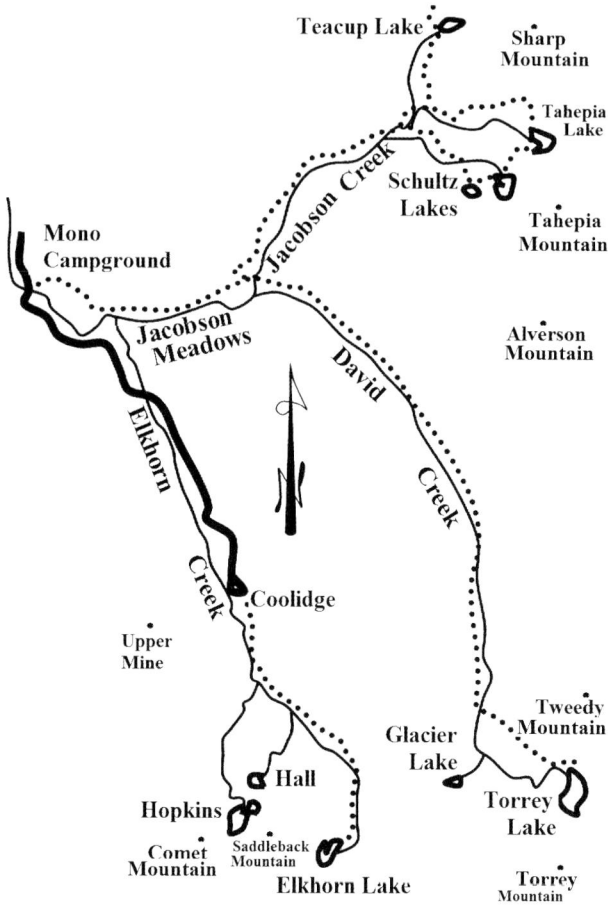

the road toward the old town of Coolidge for two miles (3.2 km) to the south side of Jacobson Meadows. This maneuver will save a 1.5-mile (2.4 km) walk and some elevation change, but it may also require getting feet wet when fording the stream or while walking through wet grass. Park the vehicle and drop to the south side of the long meadow. There's no trail here; walk along the south side of Jacobson Meadows to the east end before crossing the stream, possibly by wading. After crossing the stream, hikers can travel either toward Tahepia Lake or toward Torrey Lake. Riders on horseback could also travel up the south side of Jacobson Meadows to save a little distance and time.

At times, Jacobson Creek in the meadows holds fish, but at other times the fish are completely absent. Often the fish are killed by the turbulent and cold spring runoff in June. An occasional beaver pond would be nice to slow the water down and also to provide a sanctuary for fish during spring runoff and later in the summer.

I have found flakes of flint along the trail on the north side of Jacobson Meadows, and I can imagine that 200 years ago, Native Americans camped on either or both sides of the meadow. They would have supplemented their diet of roots, fish, and beaver with an occasional moose or elk. A buffalo may have also wandered into the area, perhaps followed by a grizzly bear. For defense, I would rather have had a .50-caliber Hawken than a flint-tipped arrow. In this present age, for safety reasons, pepper spray would definitely be the better protection option.

TEACUP LAKE

Teacup Lake (45°34'06"N 112°59'49"W) is a small, shallow, and fishless pond west of the open rocky ridge of Sharp Mountain. At 8,950 feet (2,728 m), Teacup Lake requires a 6.5-mile (10 km) hike with an elevation gain of 2,000 feet (610 m) from Mono Campground. After arriving at Teacup Lake, do not miss the opportunity to climb another 0.5 mile (0.8 km) and 450 feet (137 m) to the pass leading down to Crescent Lake. The additional climb is steep and possibly dangerous for horses. The pass provides an outstanding panoramic view to the north overlooking Crescent and Abundance Lakes. Very few people will ever enjoy this outstanding view.

The last time I climbed this ridge, I was rewarded with a yellow Mountain Goosefoot Violet. This flower grew in dry, gravelly soil near the top of the ridge above Teacup Lake far from its expected habitat near a stream or lake in wet ground.

Teacup Lake seldom sees visitors. A person could stay at the lake for perhaps the entire summer without seeing anyone else. On the north side of the pass, Crescent Lake receives far more attention. Elk frequent the large wooded meadow near Teacup Lake. Horses would find sufficient grass.

From Mono Campground, follow the trail east 5.5 miles (8.9 km) climbing 1,000 feet (305 m) to a trail that branches right to Schultz Lakes. Continue hiking left toward Tahepia Lake for a short distance, crossing two streams flowing from the north. The trail to Teacup Lake branches north and up the hill beside the second stream crossing. This seldom-used portion of the trail can be difficult to locate. Most of the steep, grassy slope has open timber, where hikers and horses can climb. From the last trail division, the route climbs a steep 1,000 feet (305 m) in a short distance of one mile (1.6 km). I like the trail and slope as it is, but those with horses would prefer some trail improvements.

Below is a view of Crescent and Abundance Lakes from the pass above Teacup Lake. Black Lion Mountain South dominates the

Crescent and Abundance Lakes, July 21, 2009

background with Black Lion Mountain North in the distance to the right side. Black Lion Lake is on the west side of the mountain between the two tall peaks. Grace Lake is just east of Black Lion Mountain South. The peak on the left side of the photograph shadows Maurice Mountain to the north.

TAHEPIA LAKE

Tahepia Lake (45°33'11"N 112°58'40"W), located in an alpine setting at timberline, 8,950 feet (2,728 m) in elevation, is just north of Tahepia Mountain. Anglers would enjoy this beautiful lake for its big fish, and fishing access is easy from most points around the shore even though the north edge may be soggy well into August. On one of my visits, I noticed a small, brown hummingbird visiting flowers on the south side of the lake.

The eight-mile (13 km) walk offers an elevation gain of 2,000 feet (610 m). From Mono Campground, hike 5.5 miles (8.9 km) up the trail up to where it branches southeast to Schultz Lakes. The elevation gain to this point is 1,000 feet (305 m). Take the left fork. The trail steepens, gaining another 1,000 feet (305 m) over the next 2.5 miles (4 km). A second route to Tahepia Lake, passes the two Schultz Lakes, making this a slightly longer trek but with the same elevation gain.

Waukena Lake is over the ridge to the east from Tahepia Lake. The trail extends from Mono Campground to Brownes Lake to the east for a distance of 17 miles (27 km). This trail is used by horse traffic, even though the trail over the pass above Tahepia Lake may be difficult for horses.

On the following page is a view of Tahepia Lake with Tahepia Mountain (10,473 feet, 3,192 m) in the background. Tahepia Mountain is only one mile (1.6 km) south of the lake but 1,600 feet (488 m) higher in elevation. The steep east face of Tahepia Mountain is west of Waukena Lake. Also, check the three-dimensional view by using Google Earth.

Tahepia Lake and Tahepia Mountain, July 10, 2009

SCHULTZ LAKES

The two Schultz Lakes are located a mile (1.6 km) south down the ridge from Tahepia Lake. Both lakes are in a beautiful setting with a generous flow of water providing good fishing. They are shallow along the edges, and provide both anglers and the occasional bald eagle with good opportunities. Children could wade in the shallow water as their parents prepare camp near the old cabin. I would expect that families with horses would appreciate these two lakes. In early July, the fish gather at the outlet streams. The first, western-most Lower Schultz Lake is at an elevation of 8,500 feet (2,591 m), and the second lake is at 8,700 feet (2,652 m). A couple of moose may browse in the timber south of the Lakes.

From Mono Campground, follow a trail for 5.5 miles (8.9 km) with an elevation gain of 1,000 feet (305 m). The trail branches with the north branch leading to Tahepia Lake, and the south branch of the trail crosses Jacobson Creek to Schultz Lakes. The first Schultz Lake

(45°32'47"N 112°59'30"W) is one mile (1.6 km) with an elevation gain of 600 feet (183 m) from the trail forks. The second Schultz Lake (45°32'48"N 112°59'04"W) is another mile (1.6 km) along the trail with an elevation gain of an additional 200 feet (61 m). From Upper Schultz Lake, a trail leads up to Tahepia Lake.

On May 24, 1997, I used snowshoes to hike into Lower Schultz Lake to catch a few fish at the inlet stream. Ice and snow covered the lake, and the inlet stream flowed through a five-foot (1.5 m) canyon of snow. At that time, crossing the swift Jacobson Creek at the bottom of the hill on a bridge of snow was a little uncertain. Now there is a manmade bridge.

Below is a view of Lower Schultz Lake (West) looking southeast with Mount Alverson (10,467 feet, 3,190 m) in the background beyond the more prominent unnamed peak in this view. Alverson Mountain can be climbed from Schultz Lakes, but the climb from Tendoy Lake to the east is easier with an elevation gain of 1,200 feet (366 m).

Lower Schultz Lake, July 10, 2009

TORREY LAKE

Torrey Lake (45°28'08"N 112°58'14"W) is located at 8,960 feet (2,731 m) elevation in a beautiful alpine setting north of Torrey Mountain (11,147 feet, 3,397 m). Tweedy Mountain (11,154 feet, 3,399 m) is one mile (1.6 km) to the north and 2,200 feet (671 m) higher than Torrey Lake. This lake is both large and deep, providing good fishing, but by the time you walk to the lake and back out in the same day, little time for fishing remains. Torrey Lake is a bad place to twist an ankle because the four-hour walk then turns into a seven-hour walk, one way. Because of the long hike, I have slept in the truck for an early start. Plentiful grass grows here for horses on an overnight stay at the lake. In the past, four-wheelers and trail bikes were permitted after midsummer and could travel within two miles (3.2 km) of the lake, parking at the bottom of the hill before the last stream crossing.

On one of my trips to Torrey Lake, a young college student accompanied me. Since the hike was long, I suggested that he walk ahead to have more time to fish; but when I arrived the student was not there. After remaining at the lake for a couple of hours, I slowly returned back down the trail hoping to find my lost friend. I was resting on the trail when he finally caught up. His story was that he had followed an old unused path while I had passed him on the new trail. This was the same student who fell into Ferguson Lake head first while trying to take a picture of the big fish. It is hard to believe that someone would fall into the water while trying to take a picture, but in the early 1980s, I fell into Rock Creek downstream from Brownes Lake. I was also taking pictures, and as I slipped from the rock, I grabbed a brush. The water was so strong that I was skipping on top of the water rather than sinking and even my antique Exakta camera was not very wet. By using the brush as an anchor, I slowly pulled myself up to solid ground. I earned an education on the serious danger of swiftly flowing streams.

From Mono Campground, Torrey Lake is nine miles (14 km) with an elevation gain of 2,000 feet (610 m). The trail branches at two miles (3.2 km) from Mono Campground with the north branch going on to Tahepia Lake and the south branch continuing up David Creek to Torrey Lake. There is an 800-foot (244 m) elevation gain in the last two miles (3.2 km).

Below is a view of Torrey Lake with Torrey Mountain in the background to the south. Upper Bond Lake is on the other side of the low pass on the ridge east of Torrey Mountain. Barb Lake is over the mountain to the east of Torrey Lake.

Torrey Lake and Torrey Mountain, July 30, 2010

GLACIER LAKE

Glacier Lake (45°28'07"N 112°59'37"W) is a most beautiful lake and one of my favorites. Glacier Lake is located two miles (3.2 km) northwest of Torrey Lake on a steep, rocky bench. The lake is actually a large pond with no fish, although the extra effort is well worth the long, steep climb. After reaching this lake, rest and relax against a rock while eating lunch and enjoying the tremendous view of Tweedy Mountain to the east. A few rock climbers explore the vertical rock face on the side of and a little south of Tweedy Mountain. Very few people will ever visit Glacier Lake.

To get to Glacier Lake, continue up the trail toward Torrey Lake after the last stream crossing. After gaining some elevation and distance toward Torrey Lake (approximately one mile, 3.2 km), leave the trail and cut back toward the stream that comes down from Glacier Lake. Climb up the steep drainage near the stream but avoid venturing far from the outlet stream since steep, rocky slopes and cliffs block the way. Both pink and white Pygmy Bitterroot flowers bloom during early August near the lake. The total distance and elevation change are about the same as that to Torrey Lake. A few people have hiked from the town of Coolidge up Elkhorn Creek and over the ridge to Glacier Lake. While this approach is actually shorter than walking up David Creek, a very steep ridge crossing impedes the route.

Glacier Lake and Tweedy Mountain, July 30, 2010

The last time that I visited Glacier Lake, a large, truck-sized rock crashed down the steep avalanche chute near the outlet stream. Numerous smaller rocks and dust ensued. I stood in the bottom path of that avalanche area an hour earlier.

On the previous page is a view of Glacier Lake with Tweedy Mountain to the east. Gorge Lakes are slightly north of Tweedy Mountain, and Barb Lake is slightly south and east of the peak.

THE OLD TOWN OF COOLIDGE

The old town of Coolidge is 25 miles (40 km) south of the town of Wise River and requires a 0.5-mile (0.8 km) walk from the parking area to the town. Yellow-bellied marmots live under the foundations of the old buildings. The grizzled rodents whistle at visitors. A few mosquitoes may buzz out to visit too.

ELKHORN LAKE

Elkhorn Lake (45°27'31"N 113°01'07"W), a medium-sized lake at 8,700 feet (2,652 m), offers good fishing at times. Elkhorn Lake is located just south of Saddleback Mountain. Actually, Saddleback Mountain has two east ridges, but only the taller peak can be seen from Coolidge and from some points farther north. Elkhorn Lake is around the south side of that second ridge. At one time, considerable downed timber cluttered the last mile of travel forcing hikers to crawl over logs to arrive at the lake. A microburst in August 1941 resulted in the deadfall. The steep path up to the lake now provides much easier access.

The four-mile (6.4 km) hike has an elevation gain of 1,300 feet (396 m). Most of the trail meanders up the valley along the east side of Elkhorn Creek. The last mile of the hike includes a steep trail on the north side and beside the stream from Elkhorn Lake. The trail leading up the hill may be difficult to locate, but in recent years the trail has seen more foot traffic and is easier to discover. The stream flows down the hill between two buttresses, one to the north and one to the south. The hillside south of the stream has no downed timber but is steep in places.

The lake can also be reached from the west past Dingley Lake and then by climbing over the ridge. Another approach is the climb up the steep ridge above Hopkins Lake, west of Saddleback Mountain.

Another favorable hike follows Elkhorn Creek to its very source. The first half of the hike follows a good trail, but no trail exists for the trip's second half. Elk reside in the upper Elkhorn Creek drainage and possibly a few mountain goats live near the mountaintops. The north end of Sawtooth Mountain can be climbed from the upper Elkhorn Creek area, but a better approach would be to climb up from Anchor Lake to the east for an elevation gain of 1,100 feet (335 m).

Below is a view of Saddleback Mountain near the town of Coolidge. Elkhorn Lake is one mile (1.6 km) south of the saddle. Hall Lake is on

Saddleback Mountain, July 15, 2008

the north side just under the tall peak, and Hopkins Lake is just west of the tall peak.

HOPKINS AND HALL LAKES

Hopkins and Hall Lakes are located just north of Saddleback Mountain and east of Comet Mountain. (Hopkins Lake is at approximately 45°27'51"N 113°02'12"W.) Both lakes occur in an exceptionally beautiful setting, backdropped by Comet Mountain. The larger and deeper Hopkins Lake provides better fishing than Hall Lake. In fact, I've encountered no fish on most trips to Hall Lake, but the last few times that I visited, I found a lively population of cutthroat trout. On one of my mid-June hikes, Hall Lake remained nearly covered with ice. At that time, I saw no fish in the lake, but I noticed a fat, four-inch- (10 cm) long salamander swimming near the bottom. The large salamander apparently did not need to hide from fish at that time. That same day, I spotted a large billy goat lying on a rock at the top of the mountain above the ice-covered Hopkins Lake. By the time I had climbed Saddleback Mountain, the goat had left. The south side and the west end of Hopkins Lake present good places for fly-fishing because no trees or brush will snag a back cast.

In the past, my preferred route to the lakes included a walk past the old town of Coolidge up the meandering trail to the east end of Saddleback Mountain before leaving the trail to climb the steep ridge to Hall Lake first and then on to Hopkins Lake, 0.5 mile (0.8 km) to the west. The climb requires a four-mile (6.4 km) walk with an elevation gain of 1,500 feet (457 m).

A second approach to the two lakes begins from the Upper Mine. Drive around the north end of Comet Mountain to the Upper Mine above the town of Coolidge. Follow an old constructed path (45°29'18"N 113°02'42"W) for a short distance down the hill from the mine to the bench that leads along the ridge. On my last trip, I followed a faint path along the bench to the north side of the stream from Hopkins Lake. I was able to follow the path to just down the hill from Hopkins Lake. In the future, the path will probably be used more and will be easier to follow. This approach required a two-mile (3.2 km) hike and an elevation change of 900 feet (274 m). Much of the elevation will be gained within the last 0.5 mile (0.8 km) of travel.

Another approach to the two lakes begins from the west past Dingley Lake and over a very steep, rocky slope to Hopkins Lake. A few folks drive high on the west slope of Comet Mountain to the Gar Mine and then walk around the mountain. The drive up the steep, narrow road has several switchbacks, more appropriate for four-wheeler traffic than for a full-sized vehicle. The old mine is located high above timberline at 9,500 feet (2,896 m) with great panoramic views of the town of Polaris, the upper Grasshopper Creek area, Maverick Mountain ski slopes, and the Crystal Park area. The Gar Mine rests at the same elevation as the pass leading down to Hopkins Lake. When hiking from the Gar Mine

Hopkins Lake and Comet Mountain, July 15, 2008

to the pass, one should drop down in elevation slightly to have fewer large boulders and more grass for the one-mile (1.6 km) hike. Avoid this approach during potential lightning storms.

On the previous page is a view from the pond east of Hopkins Lake with the beautiful Comet Mountain in the background. One day while I fished with a friend, I made the 600-foot (183 m) climb up the ridge to the pass. The climb is fairly easy, but requires care on the steep slope. The main part of Hopkins Lake hides just beyond the trees.

MOUNTAIN GOAT

High on the top of the cliff rocks,
the mountain goat she walks

Stops for awhile on a large stone,
looks down and then walks on

Surveying the cliff and rocks below for other goats
or for danger I suppose

A small kid obediently follows behind;
they disappear to reappear at a later time

The eyesight of a goat is strong
and she can see me clearly if I am not wrong

At Hopkins Lake I slump against a tree
using good binoculars in order to see

Finally they disappear over the narrow ridge;
I continue to watch but they do not return.

In the past I climbed those rocks late one morning,
a large billy lay on a promontory

The billy watched patiently the ice covered wall.
I climbed slowly to avoid a fall.

When finally the ridgetop I reach,
the billy had tracked south along another ridge

I stood for a while enjoying the view:
Hopkins, Hall, and Coolidge below.

poem continued on page 118

Through deep snow drifts to Elkhorn Lake,
at the edge of the ice a few stunted fish to take.

Since the fishing was so poor I left very soon,
returned to the truck a little after noon.

Nanny Mountain Goat, July 15, 2008

TRAIL TO DINGLEY LAKE

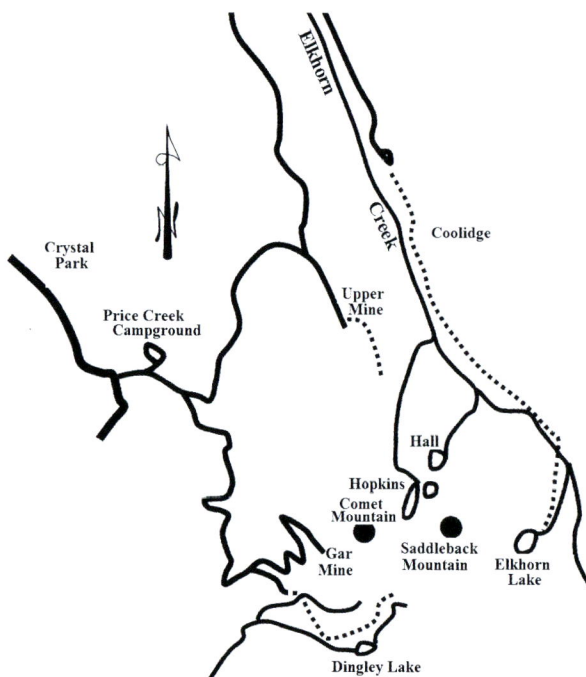

DINGLEY LAKE

Dingley Lake (45°26'50"N 113°02'42"W) is a small lake located in a beautiful valley just south of Comet Mountain. A large stream enters and leaves the lake, providing fresh water for the few fish. On my last trip, several small brook trout swam past. Two campfire rings indicated goat hunters camped in the fall or snowmobilers warmed up during winter. This drainage usually sprouts wildflowers and perhaps some fresh goat footprints with tuffs of white hair attached to the brush. I suspect that most of the goats will be nannies, some with babies. The eyes of some goats are exceptionally beautiful, perhaps more beautiful than the big cats'. The serious goat hunter should have a small camera to remember the hunt and to take a picture of the eyes for the taxidermist. By mid-November, mountain goats dress up in their long winter coats.

The road to the lake turns east one mile (1.6 km) south of Crystal Park. Turn just before going down the hill to Elkhorn Hot Springs and Polaris. Follow the road past Price Creek Campground for nearly one mile (1.6 km) before turning south from the road around the north end of Comet Mountain to the Upper Coolidge Mine. Follow this side road for three more miles (4.8 km) up the west side of Comet Mountain before parking in a steep spot (approximately 45°27'21"N 113°03'47"W), and walking around the ridge on a steep road. Avoid the temptation to drive down the steep road since it gets narrow after 100 yards (91m). The total walking distance to Dingley Lake is less than two miles (3.2 km) with an elevation change of 600 feet (183 m), an easy hike. Cross the stream at the bottom of the hill and walk up a steep trail. The lake is just off the trail to the south near the low part of the ridge. The trail has been filled with rocks and stumps to discourage the use of four-wheelers.

When I first hiked into Dingley Lake 30 years ago, there was indication of considerable horse traffic, but no sign of horses in the area existed the last time that I visited.

Below is a view of Dingley Lake looking east with the pass overlooking Hopkins Lake in the background. The small pointed peak is the west end of Saddleback Mountain. Hopkins Lake is north of that small peak, and Elkhorn Lake is located to the south a mile (1.6 km) beyond the peak in the middle of the picture.

Dingley Lake, August 18, 2009

THE PANORAMIC VIEW

The panoramic view (45°27'26"N 113°02'16"W) of Hopkins Lake shows the valley where the ghost town of Coolidge is located. The town of Coolidge is 2,000 feet (610 m) lower and Hopkins Lake is 600 feet (183 m) lower than the photo location. The bench along the mountainside above Coolidge is 600 feet (183 m) above the town site but 100 feet

(30 m) lower than the Upper Mine. When hiking to Hopkins Lake from the Upper Mine, walk along this bench to avoid the serious rock obstructions on the mountainside.

The best approach to this panoramic view is to walk past Dingley Lake. The total distance from the parking spot is three miles (4.8 km) with an elevation change of 1,100 feet (335 m). A good trail leads most of the walk. Horses and riders can access the Dingley Creek drainage to near the ridge overlook. A short hike of 100 yards (91 m) is necessary to cover the last leg to the ridge top.

Hopkins Lake, August 18, 2009

Walking a short distance to the south along the ridge leads to a second panoramic view. Elkhorn Lake appears below with both Torrey and Tweedy Mountains in the background to the east. Torrey Lake is just north of Torrey Mountain and Glacier Lake resides just over the ridge toward Tweedy Mountain in this view. The large basin west of Torrey Mountain is located over the ridge at the south side of this picture.

Elkhorn Lake with Tweedy and Torrey Mountains, August 18, 2009

TRAILS TO SAWTOOTH AND POLARIS LAKES

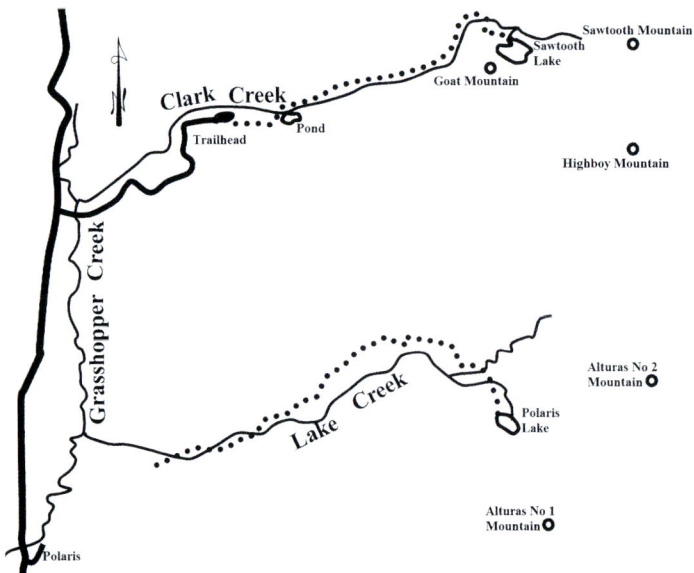

SAWTOOTH LAKE

Sawtooth Lake (45°26'00"N 113°02'01"W) is a beautiful big lake near the timberline that usually provides good fishing because the lake is not only quite deep but has a generous flow of water. Sawtooth Lake is north of Goat Mountain and south of Sawtooth Mountain, with Highboy Mountain to the southeast. Sawtooth Mountain is west of Anchor Lake, and Highboy Mountain is west of Chan Lake in the basin just west of Torrey Mountain.

July 11, 1957, a plane crashed at the southeast end of Sawtooth Lake, and parts of that wreckage remain visible. Some folks still remember helping to carry out the pilot's remains and some parts of the plane. The plane was spraying for spruce budworm infestation. As the heavy military plane turned at the south end of the lake, it hit the treetops. The crash occurred in the rocks at the south end. Most of the plane plunged into the lake. Initially the plane was secured with rope and submerged in 15 feet (5 m) of water, but over the years, it drifted deeper into the 60-foot-deep (18 m) lake.

The road to the lake turns east three miles (4.8 km) north of Polaris near Grasshopper Inn. This side road generally follows Clark Creek through a housing development for a distance of three miles (4.8 km) to a parking spot (45°25'29"N 113°05'05"W). The walk to Sawtooth Lake is three miles (4.8 km) with an elevation gain of 1,600 feet (488 m) from the trailhead, a perfect early June snowshoe hike.

A small shallow pond known as Clark Lake (45°25'27"N 113°04'25"W) exists just south of the trail one mile (1.6 km) from the trailhead. Turn off the trail for 100 yards (91 m) just before the first stream crossing. Some of the water from Clark Creek has been diverted through the pond, keeping the ten small trout alive and happy. Local children fish here, but the pond would be more productive if the water level increased a few feet.

On the following page is a view of Sawtooth Lake with Highboy

Sawtooth Lake and Highboy Mountain, June 26, 2009

Mountain in the background at a distance of one mile (1.6 km) with an elevation gain of 1,900 feet (579 m). The plane crash occurred at the far southeast end of the lake.

POLARIS LAKE

Polaris Lake (45°23'19"N 113°02'05"W), near timberline, offers reasonable fishing. The lake is shallow along most of the shore except the entire west side where the water reaches some depth. Polaris Lake is somewhat similar to Sawtooth Lake, but not quite as large and probably not nearly as deep, since Sawtooth Lake has a maximum depth of 60 feet (18 m).

Few people travel to Polaris Lake since private land crosses the route and permission is needed. Ask for permission in person after hay is cut in September and take a thank you gift with you. The trail requires a 5.5-mile (8.9 km) hike and a 1,800-foot (549 m) elevation gain. Begin the hike from near Polaris, which is located 37 miles (60 km) south of the town of Wise River and 37 miles (60 km) northwest of Dillon.

The hike over the mountain from Estler Lake to Polaris Lake would be difficult. This route would continue up Estler Creek to the pass between Alturas No. 1 and Alturas No. 2 Mountains for three miles (4.8 km) and an elevation change of 3,000 feet (914 m). The return trip would require a climb of 1,300 feet (396 m) from the lake to the pass. Those with more energy could walk over the pass just west of Dollar Lake.

The photograph below shows Polaris Lake with Alturas No. 1 Mountain to the southeast, two miles (3.2 km) distant and 2,000 feet (610 m) higher in elevation. Alturas No. 2 Mountain is two miles (3.2 km) east and Baldy Mountain is three miles (4.8 km) south of Alturas No. 1 Mountain. High ridges connect these three peaks. Scott Lake is east of Baldy Mountain and south of Alturas No. 1 Mountain in this view.

Polaris Lake and Alturas No. 1 Mountain, September 6, 2010

*

Chapter 4

ENTERING THE WEST PIONEER MOUNTAINS FROM THE SCENIC BYWAY SOUTH OF WISE RIVER

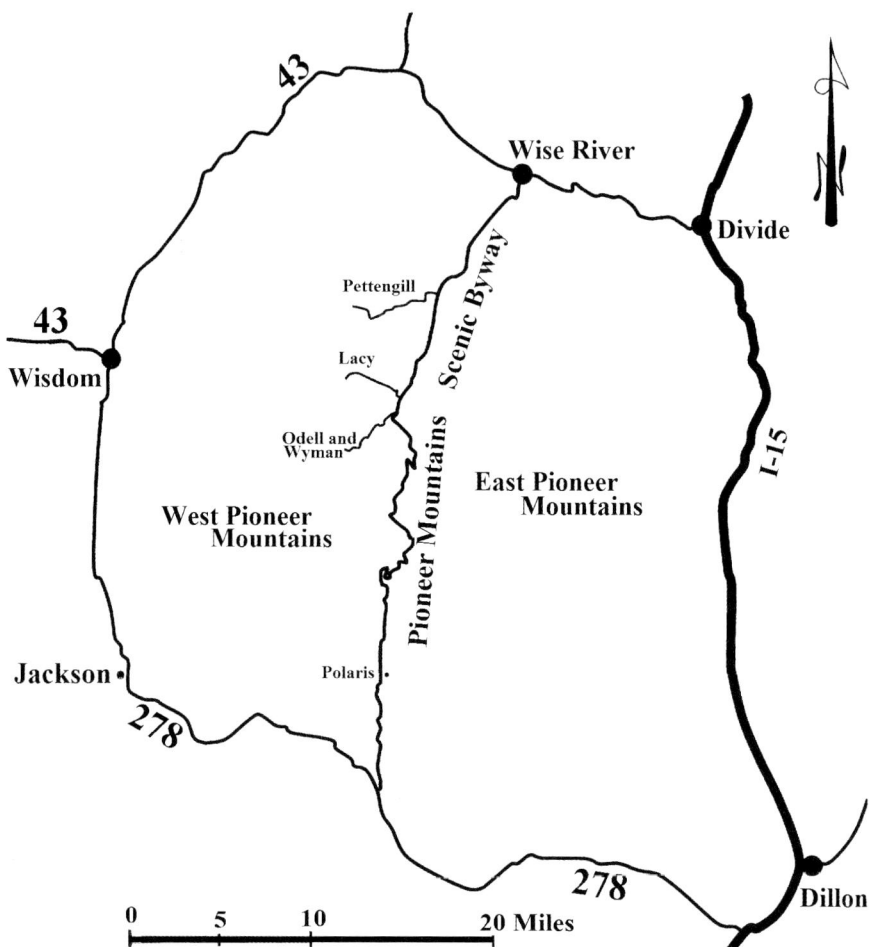

The lakes of the West Pioneer Mountains are described here beginning with lakes accessible from the Pioneer Mountains Scenic Byway, south of the town of Wise River. Lakes accessible from Pettengill, Lacy, Wyman, and Odell Creeks will be discussed in that order. Next, those lakes on the west side of the Pioneer Mountains will be described, beginning with Bryant, Christiansen, Doolittle, and Steel Creeks. Last, access to the south end of the mountains through Bull Creek Road will be considered. Twenty-five lakes dot the West Pioneer Mountains, with fourteen lakes on the east side and eleven lakes on the west side. Note that several trails appropriate for horse traffic, especially in the West Pioneer Mountains, are not described in this book.

PETTENGILL CREEK DRAINAGE

The Pettengill Creek drainage (Pattengail) is 10 miles (16 km) south of the town of Wise River. A rough road extends for 10 miles (16 km) up the drainage with horse trails branching in several directions from that main road.

The Pettengill Dam (Wise River Dam) washed out June 14, 1927, but some of the dam remnants still exist a mile (1.6 km) upstream from the confluence of Pettengill Creek and Wise River. Drive on Pettengill Road two miles (3.2 km) to the stream to find the old dam. Some folks use canoes to travel upstream from that point. The stream and valley

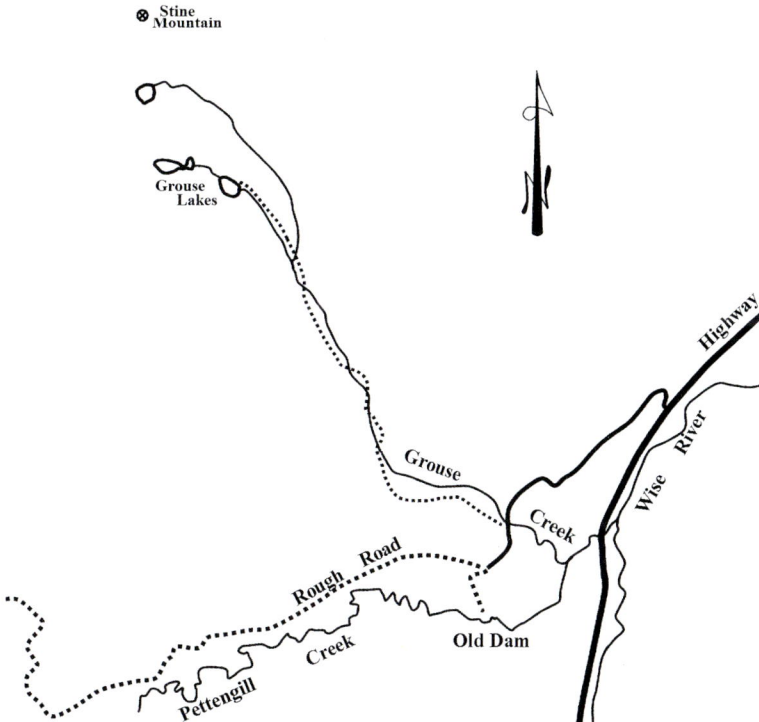

remain nearly level for two miles (3.2 km) upstream from the dam.

The road up the Pettengill drainage continues for another seven miles (11 km) from the old dam to a nice camping area at the end of the road. The remainder of the road is unimproved and most folks avoid the effort. The road becomes rough, narrow, and one lane for a short distance. A rough, rocky 500-yard (457 m) slope crossing prohibits most vehicles. Four-wheelers use the route during fall elk hunts. For most of the drainage, fishing is either poor or nonexistent. If a few beavers would build small dams, that would raise the water table and provide better fishing, better grass, and a place for birds to raise families. The few people camping at the end of the road feel that it is their camping area. The rough road keeps most people out.

GROUSE LAKES

The three Grouse Lakes are located just to the south of Stine Mountain, the tallest peak in the West Pioneer Mountains at 9,490 feet (2,893 m). The fishing is poor to nonexistent in the first two lakes, and the third and higher lake has no fish but may have numerous trophy class mosquitoes that fight for a place to land. All three lakes are shallow and the fish may freeze out during the extended winter. The challenging day hike rewards visitors with three nice alpine lakes.

Drive up the Pettengill road one mile (1.6 km) to three cabins. A narrow, rough parking spot exists near the small Grouse Creek drainage (45°41'01"N 113°04'25"W). Begin the climb west of the three cabins. The trail is steep up to the lower lake, requiring a 1,800-foot (549 m) climb over three miles (4.8 km). The middle Grouse Lake is up a steep drainage with no trail from the north end of the lower lake. The third lake is north and east up an open rocky slope to a small pass from the second lake. The third lake drains east and joins the stream from the other two lakes farther down the mountain. The third Grouse Lake is just under Stine Mountain at 8,650 feet (2,637 m). Reaching it

Shrubby Penstemon, July 28, 2009

requires a total hike of four miles (6.4 km) with an elevation gain of 2,300 feet (701 m) from the trailhead. On my last visit, I walked from the first lake up through the timber to the third lake before returning to the middle lake.

A few years ago in late July, I found a special flower, the Shrubby Penstemon. The flower grew on the slope above the middle lake toward the third lake. Since then, I have found this flower in several more locations, but the flowers at other locations have not been as lush or healthy as those near the Grouse Lakes.

THE LACY CREEK DRAINAGE

The Lacy Creek drainage accesses several lakes and day hikes. Drive up Lacy Creek Road for four miles (6.4 km) to the trailhead (45°36'21"N 113°10'12"W) where the parking area has plenty of space for horse trailers. Horse traffic occasionally uses the route throughout summer. Four-wheelers and trail bikers use some trails after midsummer. The trail to Schwinegar Lake is quite wide, but some of the trails are narrow and steep, permitting only horse traffic. Expect to find many wildflowers in this drainage throughout the summer. Beargrass blooms the first week of August most years.

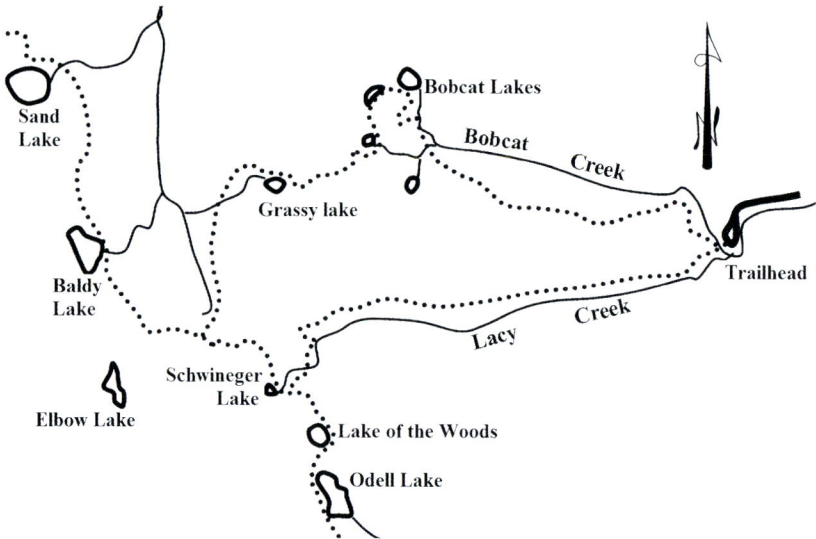

BOBCAT LAKES

The four Bobcat Lakes are located just east of Bobcat Mountain. The first and northern-most lake reached by the good horse trail usually sports a few small fish. When I first visited the lakes many years ago, the first lake had a few brook trout, but now a few small Arctic grayling survive here too. The next two lakes along the trail are called West Bobcat Lake and South Bobcat Lake. These two lakes probably lack fish. The open rock face above the second lake may spawn avalanches during

Pika, September 25, 2009

winter. The fourth lake or pond does not have fish, but does feature water critters, salamanders, bear footprints in the mud, and pika in the rocks east of the lake.

From the trailhead on Lacy Creek, the trail immediately crosses Bobcat Creek and branches north up the hill. The stream runs full in June, making for wet boots. The trail continues to climb steeply for two miles (3.2 km) before it drops again into the Bobcat Creek drainage. The climb to Bobcat Lake North (45°37'19"N 113°13'15"W) requires a four-mile (6.4 km) hike over 2,000 feet (610 m) of elevation changes— up and down. Bobcat Lakes West and South are along the trail about 0.5 mile (0.8 km) apart. The fourth lake or pond is spaced another 0.5 mile (0.8 km) through the timber with no trail to the east from South Bobcat Lake. Steep rocky ridges surround much of the fourth lake.

Below is a view of the fourth Bobcat Lake with Bobcat Mountain in the background to the northwest. The other three Bobcat Lakes line the

Fourth Bobcat Lake and Bobcat Mountain, July 20, 2010

rocky face below the mountain. Bobcat Mountain can be seen from the paved road just before the turnoff to Lacy Creek. Grassy Lake is over the small pass to the west from South Bobcat Lake.

GRASSY LAKE

Grassy Lake (45°36'38"N 113°14'33"W) is really a medium-sized pond with marshy ground around the edges. Riders rest their horses after crossing the hill from the Bobcat Lakes. Grassy Lake's location over the ridge west of Bobcat Lake South unfolds at a distance of one mile (1.6 km) with an increase of 400 feet (122 m) followed by a 400-foot (122 m) loss of elevation. The lake is three miles (4.8 km) east of Baldy Lake.

The last time I visited Grassy Lake, I hiked toward Bobcat Lakes. After hiking for two miles (3.2 km), I left the trail at ridge top and continued up the ridge, missing the lakes. I took the picture of Bobcat Mountain from the ridge above the fourth lake and rejoined the trail again above the Bobcat Lake South. When I left Grassy Lake, I turned south and hiked over the hill through the timber for one mile (1.6 km) to join the trail to Schwinegar Lake.

Grassy Lake, July 20, 2010

On the previous page is a view of Grassy Lake looking west toward Odell Mountain to the west.

I took the following photo of Odell Mountain from Bobcat Mountain just east and south of Grassy Lake. Odell Mountain (9,405 feet, 2,867 m) is the second tallest mountain in the West Pioneers. In this picture, the mountain runs nearly south to north with the highest part of the mountain at the southern end. The trail from the south end of the mountain runs north along the top of the ridge to Sand Lake. A more frequently used trail runs from Odell Lake north to Sand Lake, connecting all of the lakes except Elbow Lake. Odell Lake sits at the south end of the mountain or at the left edge of this photograph. Lake of the Woods is 0.5 mile (0.8 km) north of Odell Lake, and Schwinegar Lake hides just under the rocky outcrop near the south end of the mountain. Elbow Lake is near the middle of the picture or just north of the small peak. Baldy Lake resides just under the ridge at the north end of this photograph, with Sand Lake beyond the picture edge, two miles (3.2 km) north of Baldy Lake.

Odell Mountain, July 20, 2010

SCHWINEGAR LAKE

Schwinegar Lake (45°35'15"N 113°14'36"W), a small, spring-fed lake, harbors hundreds of grayling eager to catch a fly. By mid-August, grayling become inactive and apparently take a nap. Even though the lake is small in area, its depth provides a generous flow of water. The lake is 4.5 miles (7.2 km) with an elevation gain of 1,350 feet (411 m) from the trailhead on Lacy Creek.

Schwinegar Lake, September 14, 2010

ELBOW LAKE

Elbow Lake (45°35'15"N 113°16'10"W) is a large, beautiful lake east of Odell Mountain ridge at an elevation of 8,660 feet (2,640 m). This lake's size seems to encourage fishing, but the lack of fish may be due to the lack of water flowing through the lake. No definite stream enters or leaves the lake. The large meadow at the south end of the lake should provide sufficient grass for horses for a week of camping.

Elbow Lake, located through the timber, offers no trail beginning at the north side of Schwinegar Lake. The additional climb is 2.5 miles (4.0 km) with elevation gain of 500 feet (152 m). The total hike from the trailhead on Lacy Creek is seven miles (11 km) with an elevation gain of 1,800 feet (549 m). The first time I visited Elbow Lake, I hiked to Baldy Lake and then turned south through the timber. Below is a view of Elbow Lake with the small peak on Odell Mountain in the background to the south.

Elbow Lake, July 29, 2009

BALDY LAKE

Baldy Lake (45°36'11"N 113°16'20"W) is another large and beautiful lake at 8,560 feet (2,609 m) elevation with good fishing. Exceptionally deep at 85 feet (26 m), Baldy Lake has a large surface area and a generous flow of water. Disadvantages include little time to fish after walking into Baldy Lake if planning a one-day trip. An overnight camping trip may be appropriate. An open ridge on the west harbors a snowdrift into early August. One year, an abundance of Beargrass decorated the east shore.

Baldy Lake is three miles (4.8 km) north of Schwinegar Lake, three miles (4.8 km) west of Grassy Lake and two miles (3.2 km) south of Sand Lake. Good trails connect these lakes. From the Lacy Creek trailhead to Baldy Lake is seven miles with an elevation gain of 1,700 feet (518 m).

One morning as I neared Baldy Lake, a medium-sized black bear rushed toward me parallel to the path. It paused a short distance from me before it ran away. Later I tried to analyze what had happened and if I had been in any danger. As the bear ran, it made a raking noise in the brush, and I supposed that the elk hunters that were in the area had shot it with an arrow. Later in the day I noticed bear tracks along the trail to Baldy Lake and then on toward Sand Lake. Most bears will probably die of such a wound.

Below is a view of Baldy Lake looking south with the south end of Odell Mountain in the background. A light snow covers the mountain in mid-September. The deepest part of the lake is along the west side, and that deep water probably provides the best fishing. Families of pika live in the rocks and make a chirping noise when disturbed and even when not disturbed.

Baldy Lake and Odell Mountain, September 14, 2010

LAKE OF THE WOODS

Lake of the Woods (45°34'58"N 113°14'07"W) is a small lake, but it is exceptionally deep with good fishing at times for 12-inch (30 cm) trout. It is located 0.5 mile (0.8 km) south of Schwinegar Lake or 0.5 mile (0.8 km) north of Odell Lake. The four-wheeler trail to Lake of the Woods stops short of the steep downhill path to Odell Lake's shore. The entire area surrounding the Lake of the Woods westward to Stewart Meadows and south to Upper Anderson Meadows attracts many elk and has good elk habitat. Hunters in these areas may encounter other hunters.

One summer, I hiked through the timber east of Lake of the Woods. I remained in the timber for five miles on the ridge south and above Lacy Creek. If I wanted another place to elk hunt, I would become familiar with this area. I enjoy those places where I need to climb 1,000 feet (305 m) to find good hunting.

Following is a view of Lake of the Woods looking north. Many fish were rising the day that I took this picture.

Lake of the Woods, July 25, 2009

ODELL LAKE

Odell Lake (45°34'40"N 113°14'08"W), large and deep, features both grayling and trout. Until ten years ago, only grayling survived in the lake, but now both grayling and trout compete for a fly or spinner. Odell Lake, is located 0.5 mile (0.8 km) south of the Lake of the Woods and down a steep trail. Odell Lake is five miles (8.0 km) from the trailhead on Lacy Creek with an elevation increase of 1,500 feet (457 m) and an elevation loss of 200 feet (61 m).

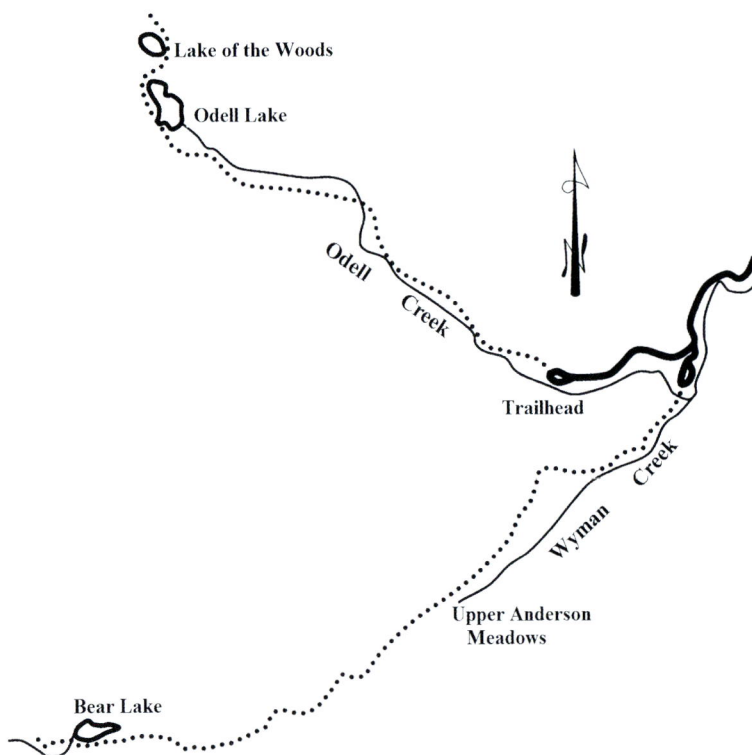

A shorter hike to Odell Lake begins from the trailhead on Odell Creek (45°32'50"N 113°10'17"W). Drive up the Wyman Creek drainage for 4.5 miles (7.2 km) on a good dirt road to a large parking area, which has a toilet and space for horse trailers. From the trailhead, the hike travels four miles (6.4 km) on a horse trail with an elevation gain of 1,000 feet (305 m).

Actually, the route up Odell Creek past Odell Lake to Lake of the Woods would be 4.5 miles (7.2 km) with an elevation gain of 1,200 feet (366 m) while the distance from the Lacy Creek trailhead is also 4.5 miles (7.2 km) with an elevation gain of 1,500 feet (457 m). Both routes to Lake of the Woods are similar except that four-wheelers may use the trail from the Lacy Creek trailhead. Those with four-wheelers often admit that much of the trail is rough.

Below is a view of Odell Lake with the southeast end of Odell Mountain in the background. One year, ice and snow covered Odell Lake, at 8,350 feet (2,545 m) elevation, on June 9.

Odell Lake, July 25, 2009

BEAR LAKE

Bear Lake (45°30'29"N 113°14'45"W) is used for irrigation and drains during July and August, providing either no fishing or poor fishing.

A seven-mile (11 km) walk includes a 500-foot (152 m) elevation change. Follow a good trail from the trailhead (45°32'56"N 113°08'58"W) on Wyman Creek at Lower Anderson Meadows. During early June, the streams fill, and the meadows become lakes; expect to get your feet wet. Also in early June, expect to find spruce grouse, sandhill cranes, porcupine, deer, elk with calves, and an occasional bear looking for elk calves. The flower, Spring Beauty, shows off in June.

Bear Lake is also south of Stewart Lake on a good trail through the timber east of Stewart Mountain. This approach requires a two-mile (3.2 km) walk from Stewart Lake. Another approach to Bear, Stewart, and Steer Lakes starts from the south by way of Bull Creek. See page 162 for this approach.

Below is a view looking west to Bear Lake in mid-June with Stewart Mountain and Deer Peak in the background. Bear Lake at 7,580 feet (2,310 m) elevation was ice free in this picture and on June 5 another year.

Bear Lake with Stewart Mountain and Deer Peak, June 12, 2010

Chapter 5

*

ENTERING THE WEST PIONEER MOUNTAINS FROM THE WEST SIDE

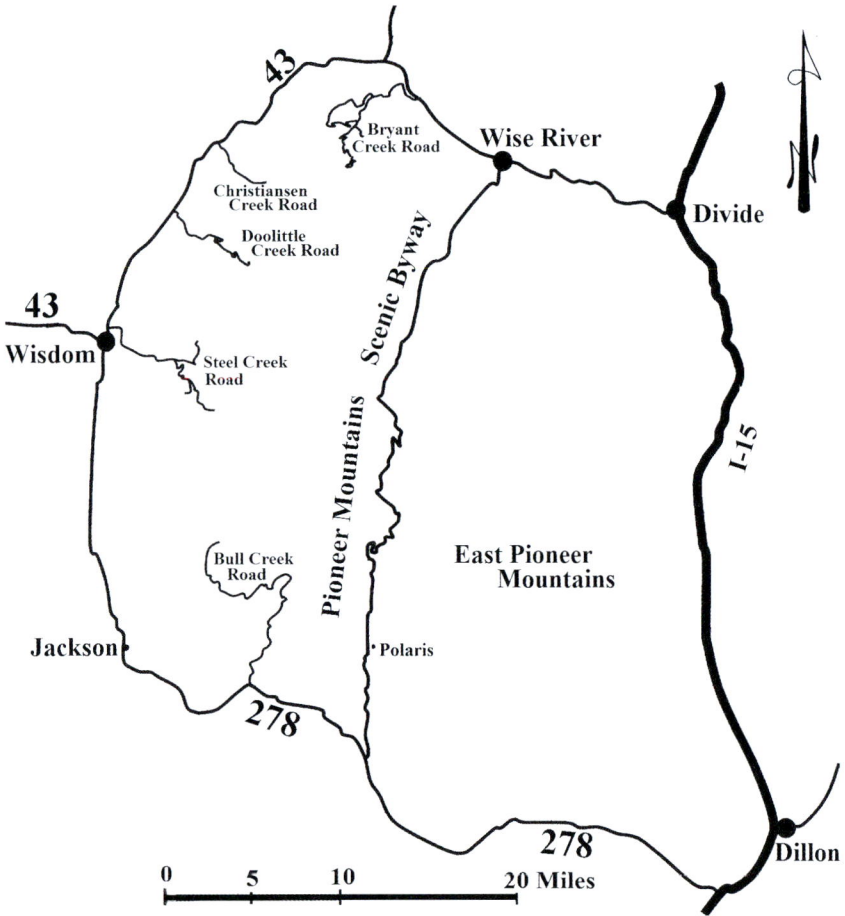

The eleven lakes on the west side of the West Pioneer Mountains will be considered beginning with Bryant, Christiansen, Doolittle, and Steel Creeks in that order. The Bull Creek Road to the south of Jackson provides a good route to Stewart Lake after the Warm Springs Creek flow decreases in August.

BRYANT CREEK ROAD

Bryant Creek Road begins at the Dickie Bridge (45°51'02"N

113°04'07"W), nine miles (14 km) west of the town of Wise River on Montana Highway 43.

Three lakes may be reached from the end of the Bryant Creek Road. Actually, all three lakes are in the Alder Creek drainage to the east but can be reached from the gated end of the Bryant Creek Road. The steel gate across the road at the top of Foolhen Ridge is 12 miles (19 km) from the Dickie Bridge on Highway 43, and the campground located near Dickie Bridge.

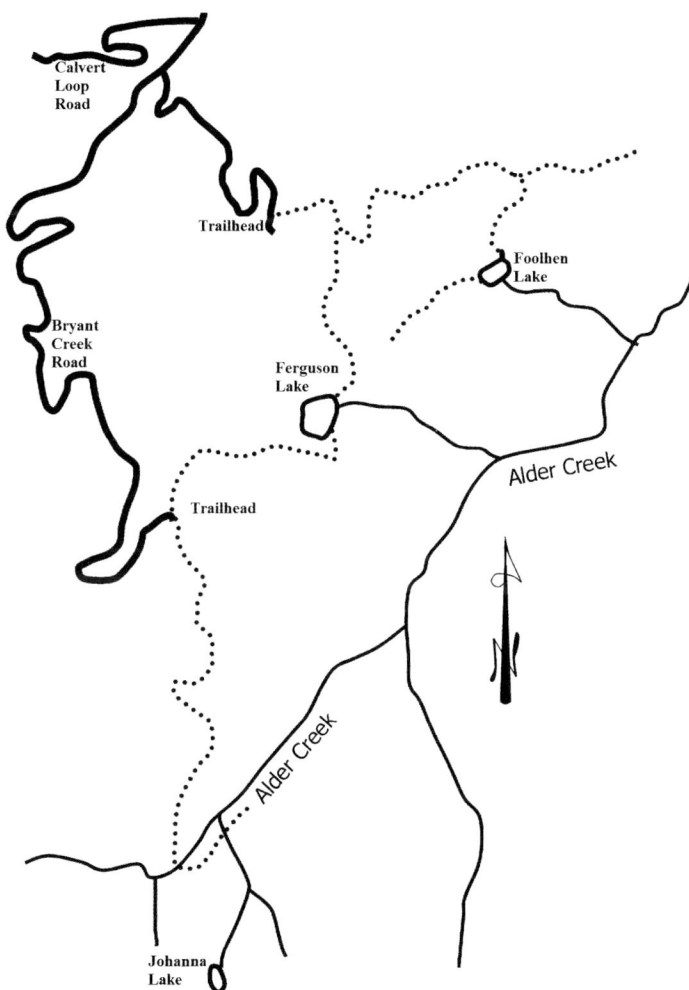

FERGUSON LAKE

Ferguson Lake (45°47'49"N 113°07'51"W) frustrates fishermen and women since the fish become most active only in late June and early July. In the morning, large cutthroat trout cruise the shore counterclockwise looking for freshwater shrimp. This lake should be fished early mornings in early July. Catch-and-release fishing or a self-imposed limit of two fish would be appropriate. After about mid-July, the fish submerge, making the lake appear barren. The 48-foot-deep (18 m) lake may have a spring entering the lake from the bottom.

A small forest fire burned the hill just north of the lake several years ago. This fire was probably caused by careless campers. Once, I recommended that one of my students try this lake. After fishing for some time without luck, he tried to take a picture of the large fish that swam by. As he knelt on the bank to focus his camera, he slipped and fell head first into the deep water. He took his Montana fishing story back to California.

Ferguson Lake, August 21, 2009

The trailhead to Ferguson Lake begins at the top of Foolhen Ridge near the steel gate. Hike north along the ridge for one mile (1.6 km) on a good four-wheeler trail. Then turn down the hill for another mile (1.6 km) to the lake. This easy two-mile (3.2 km) hike decreases in elevation 600 feet (183 m) from the trailhead.

An old, hard-to-follow trail leads west along the lake's south side and up an unmaintained trail to meet up with the other trail near the top of the hill.

On the previous page is a view of Ferguson Lake looking south from the ridge leading to Foolhen Lake to the north. The trail to Ferguson Lake travels downhill just south of the lake.

FOOLHEN LAKE

Foolhen Lake (45°48'30"N 113°06'40"W) is small but deep with water lilies growing 20 feet (6.1 m) from shore. A float tube may improve the fishing opportunities. The drainage and timber surrounding the lake encourage several varieties of wildflowers, and most of my trips to Foolhen Lake have been wildflowers hunts. One August, I found the wildflower known as Candystick on the hill west of the lake; this flower is extremely rare in the Pioneer Mountains. On another occasion, in late August, I found the smaller Fringed Gentian in the marshy ground west of the lake.

Foolhen Lake is over the ridge north of Ferguson Lake, two additional miles (3.2 km) past Ferguson Lake with an elevation gain of 600 feet (183 m) and then an elevation decrease of 600 feet (183 m). From Ferguson Lake, follow the four-wheeler trail north and up the hill. Half way up the hill on the four-wheeler trail, bear east, off trail and up the hill for 0.5 mile (0.8 km) to a small bench on the ridge. The hard-to-find trail begins at the ridgetop (45°48'14"N 113°07'21"W) and travels downhill to Foolhen Lake. This seldom-used trail is not well maintained. Another much older trail travels up the hill from Alder Creek.

A better approach to Foolhen Lake is to take the rough four-wheeler trail over the hill from Bryant Creek. At six miles (9.7 km) from Montana Highway 43, a logging road crosses Bryant Creek to the east. This logging road is just past the second entrance of the Calvert Loop Road. Drive up this side road for three miles (4.8 km) to a four-wheeler trail (45°48'44"N 113°08'23"W). The trail follows the road up the hill for 0.5 mile (0.8 km) before turning up a steep hill for one mile (1.6 km) at an elevation gain of 1,100 feet (335 m). The trail then continues around the hill and down to the lake for an additional 1.5 miles (2.4 km) and an elevation loss of 900 feet (274 m). The total hiking distance is three miles (4.8 km) with an elevation gain and loss of 2,000 feet (610 m). Road restrictions limit vehicle travel for the last portion of the road.

The view above of Foolhen Lake looks south toward Ferguson Lake. The trail south to Ferguson Lake leads up that hill. The alternate route using the four-wheeler trail descends down the hill west of the lake and north from the picture's location.

In early August one year while I searched for wildflowers, an American pine marten surprised me. The playful, kitten-sized animal

Foolhen Lake, August 21, 2009

American pine marten, August 2, 2012

came close, but since it was shielded by brush, my best picture was at some distance. When it disappeared in the tree roots a short distance from me, I quietly backed off and left it in peace.

JOHANNA LAKE

Johanna Lake (45°45'16"N 113°08'32"W) is hard to find and thus nicknamed Hidden Lake for good reason, but the logging road up Bryant Creek has made Johanna Lake more accessible. Years ago, I found Johanna Lake on the second attempt by using an aerial photograph. The small lake sits at an elevation of 8,100 feet (2,469 m). A good flow of water enters and leaves the lake. Springs probably enter under the waterline on the west side where the lake is deep. The lake was free of ice on June 14 one year.

Since this lake is small, it can be over-fished easily; a self-imposed limit of two fish would be appropriate. At times, this lake appears to be a dead lake, although few fish may be in the lake on that particular year. One summer as I was leaving the lake with no fish, a large wake of a submarine appeared to be chasing a smaller fish. On another visit, I arrived with no fishhooks. After making a hook from a small piece of wire, I was surprised when I caught a fish.

The lake is located three miles (4.8 km) from the steel gate with an elevation change of 1,200 feet (366 m). Walk past the steel gate at the top of Foolhen Ridge for two miles (3.2 km) along the old logging road. The logging road crosses Alder Creek where the bridge has been removed, and then turns back east along the ridge. Alder Creek swells in June and July and may be hard to cross. Just after the road crosses Alder Creek, start climbing up the ridge. No trail exists, but the ridge can be identified by 30-year-old clearcuts. Continue to climb up to the top of the ridge and then follow the ridge up until you can look down on the lake. Drop down a short distance to the lake.

Flowers bloom abundantly along the logging road in July, especially Lupine and Indian Paintbrush. Expect to see large snowshoe rabbits and spruce grouse. One spring along this trail, I found bear scat that contained the dewclaws of a small fawn, their favorite meal. On another trip, I saw a male of the beautiful pine grosbeak, which is usually found in the Canadian Rockies. Later that summer, I took pictures of juvenile birds as they moved quickly along the path in front of me.

Below is a view of Johanna Lake looking south. Alder Peak is one mile (1.6 km) south of Johanna Lake beyond the ridge in view and 1,000 feet (305 m) higher in elevation, while Foolhen Mountain is two

Johanna Lake, July 25, 2008

miles (3.2 km) to the west. One day (in 1984) after catching no fish, I climbed the ridge in view and found deep beds in the gravel where mountain goats had apparently stayed for the winter.

CHRISTIANSEN CREEK DRAINAGE

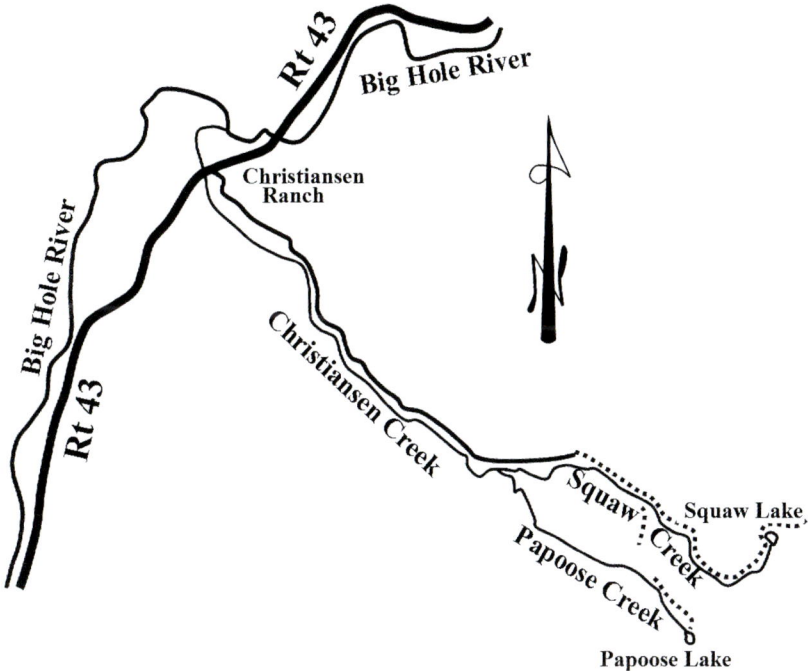

SQUAW LAKE

Squaw Lake (45°45'28"N 113°13'20"W), really a pond, is seldom fished, yet may have an occasional large fish. Elk hunters often camp on the southeast side of the lake.

The Christiansen Creek drainage is 24 miles (39 km) west of the town of Wise River and 15 miles (24 km) east from the town of Wisdom on Montana Highway 43. This drainage is just past the last bridge over the Big Hole River before arriving at Wisdom. The locked gate

Squaw Lake, September 24, 2010

at the Christiansen Ranch is open after elk season starts in the fall. A second piece of private property three miles (4.8 km) from the highway requires permission to cross. Take a thank you gift when asking for permission to cross this second parcel of ground.

Drive up the Christiansen Creek drainage for six miles (9.6 km) to the end of the road. The drive during the fall dry weather is best since serious ruts in the unmaintained road may make it impassable when wet. The easy three miles (4.8 km) to the lake travels along the east side of Squaw Creek with an elevation gain of 600 feet (183 m).

Above is a view of Squaw Lake looking southeast toward Foolhen Mountain.

PAPOOSE LAKE

Papoose Lake (45°44'41"N 113°14'12"W) supports some fish. Normally the only good reason for a person to hike to this lake would be to hunt elk. Hunters tether their horses here. You may smell elk near the top of the ridge before the lake. On my last trip, a cow elk barked at me as I climbed up through the timber. A couple of my younger friends followed a wounded cow elk for many miles through this rough country before finally killing it. The changing color of the aspen leaves makes for an exceptionally beautiful fall hike.

Park at the end of the road in the Squaw Creek drainage as if going to Squaw Lake. Climb the ridge just south of the parking spot or follow Papoose Creek up the hill. A trail near the south end of the ridgetop can be followed the last mile (1.6 km) through and around the hill to the lake. This hike will require a three-mile (4.8 km) climb and 700-foot (213 m) elevation gain.

There is also a steep trail up the ridge from Squaw Creek. Hike in toward Squaw Lake one mile (1.6 km) to a small meadow. On the far side of the meadow, the trail leads through the timber to the base of the hill. This trail will be hard to find at both the bottom and top of the ridge.

On my two trips to Squaw and Papoose Lakes, I first hiked to Squaw Lake. On the return trip back to the trailhead, I crossed Squaw Creek and climbed the ridge through the timber leading to Papoose Lake.

Papoose Lake, September 24, 2010

On my last trip to Papoose Lake, three elk hunters leading horses came over the ridge from Bible Camp Park in the upper Pettengill drainage. Apparently, an adequate horse trail leads from that direction. The guide was from Wise River, but the two bow hunters traveled from New York and were very excited to be in the mountains looking for elk. I apologized to the guide for interrupting his hunt. The guide apparently intended to remain in the area until after dark anyway.

On the previous page is a view of Papoose Lake looking southeast. The elk hunters came over the mountain from that direction. The fire from a few years ago burned down to just east of the lake.

DOOLITTLE CREEK DRAINAGE

The Doolittle Creek drainage is 30 miles (48 km) west of the town of Wise River and nine miles (14 km) east of Wisdom on Montana Highway 43. Stone Lake West and Stone Lake East may be reached from the trailhead at the end of the road up the Doolittle Creek drainage.

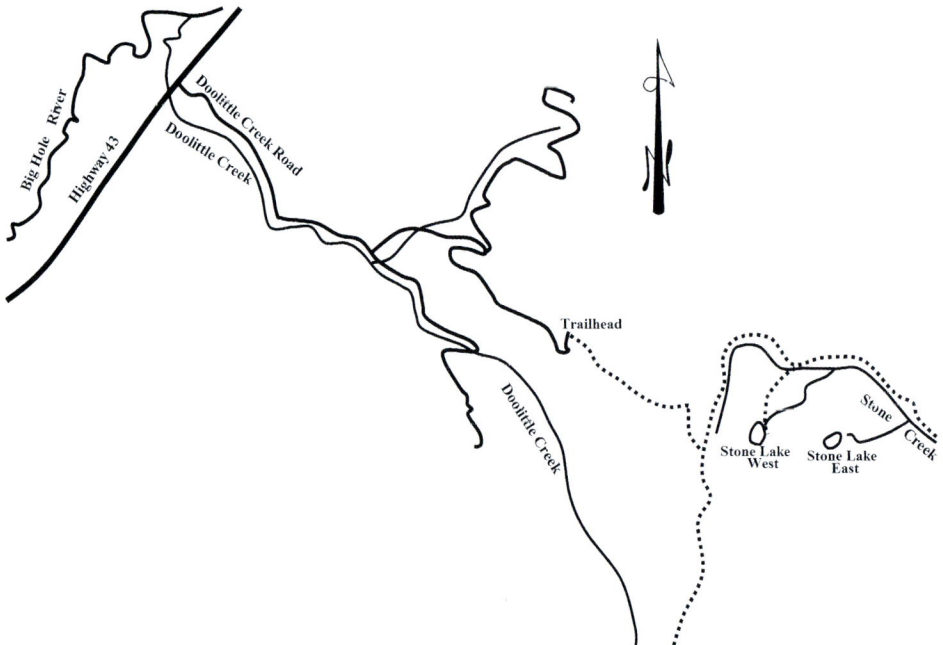

STONE LAKE WEST

Stone Lake West (45°41'23"N 113°15'26"W) is a pretty lake with a rocky slope on the west side. The lake contains a few fish, has some camping spots, and a closed four-wheeler trail. A large forest fire burned up to just east of both Stone Lakes a few years ago.

The easiest approach to the lakes is to drive up the Doolittle Creek drainage for seven miles (11 km) to the end of the road (45°42'13"N 113°17'59"W). A USDA Forest Service map would help determine which branch of dirt road to follow. The hike to Stone Lake West requires a three-mile (4.8 km) hike with an elevation change, both up and down, of 1,400 feet (427 m). Hike up the trail to the hilltop for a steep one-mile (1.6 km) climb with a 1,000-foot (305 m) elevation gain. The steep portion of the trail remains difficult, and it may be reconstructed in the future, making the trail longer but offering a more reasonable grade. From the top of the mountain, follow the trail down and around the hill to meet the trail from the Pettengill-Stone Creek drainage. Follow this new trail north for 200 yards (183 m) before leaving the trail to walk around the hill through the timber. Remain in the timber at the same elevation for a mile (1.6 km) to again meet the trail to Stone Lake West. The timber is probably open enough even for horse traffic, but a person could remain on the Pettengill-Stone Creek Trail, requiring a little more effort.

The second approach to the lakes is to drive up the Pettengill drainage road to the end (see page 129). This requires an hour drive for seven miles (13 km) over some difficult spots; borrow a friend's truck for the trip. Hike 7.5 miles (12 km) up the trail, an elevation gain of 2,000 feet (610 m). Follow the Pettengill Creek drainage for two miles (3.2 km), and then turn north on the Stone Creek drainage trail.

Stone Lake East (45°41'19"N 113°14'29"W) usually has better fishing, since it is harder to access. Stone Lake East is smaller than the first lake, but this lake is quite deep at 47 feet (14 m) with a large

East Stone Lake, July 6, 2012

flow of water. The odor of elk is often quite distinct. While no trail leads to this lake, follow around the ridge southeast to the second lake. The hike will require a one-mile (1.6 km) walk with a sharp loss in elevation of 300 feet (91 m) just west of the lake. The return trip back to the truck will require a total of 700 feet (213 m) elevation gain at the end of the day. For folks who like to fish, this lake could easily become a favorite. Above is a view of Stone Lake East looking north. Numerous fish rose to the surface the morning that I took this picture, and they were easy to catch.

ROAD TO THE STEEL CREEK DRAINAGE

The Road to the Steel Creek drainage begins just north of Wisdom. Drive up the good dirt road six miles (9.7 km) to a small parking lot near Steel Creek Campground. Part of the road may be exceptionally muddy during early spring and during wet weather. Lily Lake and Sand Lake are up the mountain to the northeast from the parking area. Stewart Meadows and Stewart Lake are on a more difficult road to the south.

Moose Meadows is located 400 feet (122 m) higher in elevation and one mile (1.6 km) southeast of Steel Creek Campground. In the early mornings, elk, moose, and an occasional bear may be in the meadow.

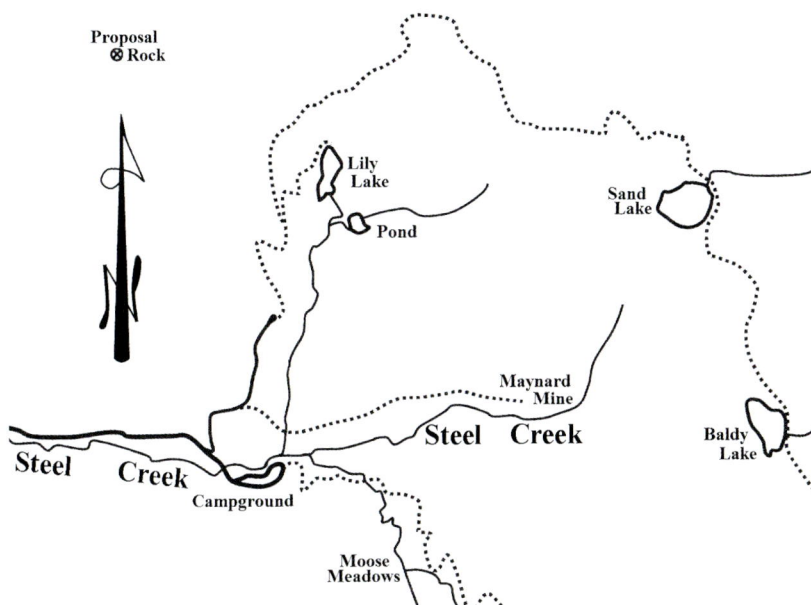

The trail to Odell Mountain continues past Moose Meadows for several more miles.

LILY LAKE WEST

Lily Lake West (45°37'30"N 113°19'42"W) in the West Pioneer Mountains is a much larger lake than Lily Lake in the East Pioneer Mountains. This larger lake occasionally provides good fishing. Drive up an unimproved, steep road north from the Steel Creek Road parking lot two miles (3.2 km) (45°36'31"N 113°20'14"W). Walk around the ridge for less than two miles (3.2 km). The elevation changes 700 feet (213 m), much of which is gained and then lost within the last 0.5 mile (0.8 km) of the hike.

I usually do not fish Lily Lake, but on September 5, 2011, I took two friends who were not used to climbing in the mountains. They felt that the steep part of the trail was difficult. We caught a few 10-inch (25 cm) fish with a spinner. On the return trip, we noticed a forest fire to

Nanny Goat with Kid, May 29, 2002

the south of our location. Later we heard that the fire was at the north end of Stewart Meadows.

One spring on May 29, I happened upon a nanny goat with a small kid on the ridge just east and above Lily Lake. When I saw the small footprint in the snow, I expected to find a baby elk calf near, but it happened to be a newborn mountain goat. I was quite close for this picture with a recyclable camera. As predators proliferate in the West Pioneer Mountains, the goat population may diminish or disappear. Lily Lake West at 7,170 feet (2,185 m) elevation was free of ice at that time.

SAND LAKE

Sand Lake (45°37'19"N 113°17'02"W) is large, quite deep (58 feet, 18 m), and has a large flow of water. The mountaintop lake at 8,280 feet (2,520 m), has the potential for good fishing and camping, especially while bow hunting. Anglers will like this lake's sandy beach on the east side.

On September 29, 2009, a fire burned the hillside east of Lily Lake and surrounding Sand Lake. I had intended to hike to Sand Lake that day, but I took a few pictures of the fire on the mountainside and returned home. The next spring on June 23, I encountered deep snowdrifts near the top of the mountain. Since I had gained so much elevation and was near the lake, I left the trail and continued through deep, wet snowdrifts to find the lake still frozen. On the return trip, I turned over the hill down Steel Creek and past the Maynard Mine.

The best approach to Sand Lake is the drive up the unimproved steep road north for two miles (3.2 km) from the Steel Creek Road and parking lot. Hike up the trail for 5.5 miles (8.9 km) and an elevation increase of 2,500 feet (762 m). The trail branches after one mile (1.6 km), with one branch leading to Lily Lake West. The upper branch continues up the ridge to Sand Lake. Some folks have used trail bikes to access the lakes.

Sand Lake is also two miles (3.2 km) north of Baldy Lake with 600

Sand Lake, September 14, 2010

feet (183 m) of up and down elevation change. The hike from the Lacy Creek trailhead to Sand Lake is 8.5 miles (14 km) with an elevation gain and loss of 2,300 feet (701 m).

A good four-wheeler trail leads up Steel Creek to the Maynard Mine (45°36'14"N 113°18'07"W), where a few log cabins in fair condition still remain. I imagine that those cabins would have exciting stories to tell. No trail from Maynard Mine to Sand Lake exists. One would need to climb another two miles (3.2 km) up the drainage with an elevation gain of 900 feet (274 m). Some of the downed timber and steep rocks may be avoided by hiking up the south side of the stream.

The Sand Lake image on the previous page looks west. The trail from the Steel Creek parking lot and trailhead comes in from the north or from the right side of the picture. The trail from Baldy Lake comes in from the south, and the trail over Odell Mountain joins the trail from Baldy Lake at 0.5 mile (0.8 km) south of Sand Lake. The forest fire from a few years ago burned most of the area west and north of the lake.

TRAIL TO STEWART LAKE

The trail to Stewart Lake begins a few miles south of Steel Creek. Drive up Steel Creek Road four miles (6.4 km) before branching south, up and around the hill. A third, seldom-used road near the top of the hill (45°35'40"N 113°21'20"W) branches east for an additional four miles (6.4 km) of difficult driving to a closed road sign and a tight parking area (45°33'36"N 113°18'37"W).

STEWART LAKE

Stewart Lake (45°31'15"N 113°16'25"W) is a small, shallow lake in the middle of the marshy Stewart Meadows just north of Stewart Mountain. At times, the fishing is good for small trout, but expect to get your feet wet since you will stand on a floating mat of grass roots.

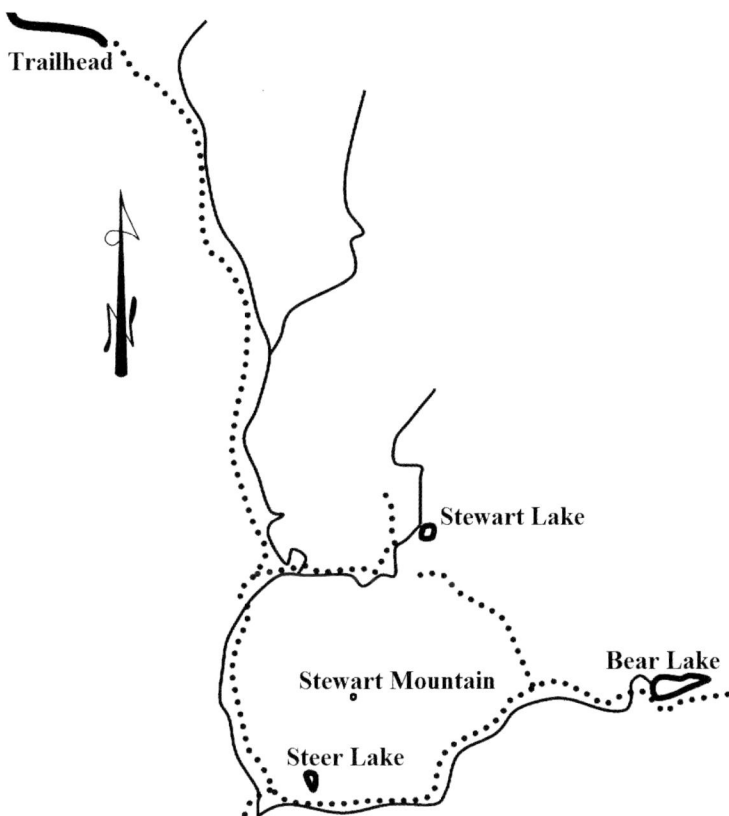

Horses cannot approach this lake because of the marshy ground and the floating mat of grass.

A more important reason to visit the Stewart Meadows area would be to manage cattle during the summer and to elk hunt in the fall. This area likely hosts several camps for much of the elk hunting season, and a person hunting in that area would likely encroach on other hunters or outfitters.

Walk south from the trailhead for 0.5 mile (0.8 km) in timber to an open meadow extending five miles (8.0 km) south and reaching the north side of Stewart Mountain. At the north side of Stewart Mountain, turn east on the east fork of Warm Springs Creek to Stewart Lake in the middle of the marshy Stewart Meadows. The total hike will require a walk of five miles (8.0 km) in an open meadow with an elevation change of 400 feet (122 m), mostly downhill. Expect to see elk during the early morning and an occasional hawk later in the day. Wildflowers are abundant in July.

A second approach to Stewart Lake is the walk past Bear Lake for another two miles (3.2 km) on a trail crossing a small pass east of Stewart Mountain. This approach requires a nine-mile (14 km) hike from the trailhead on Wyman Creek at the Lower Anderson Meadows.

Below is a view of Stewart Lake with Odell Mountain in the background to the north. Much of the meadow surrounding the lake and north of the lake is quite marshy, making for a difficult walk.

Another approach to Stewart Lake and Stewart Meadows is from the south. The Bull Creek Road is located 10 miles (16 km) southeast

Stewart Lake and Odell Mountain, July 31, 2009

of Jackson on Montana Highway 278. Drive up Bull Creek Road for 18 miles (29 km) to the private land of the Clemow Cow Camp (45°27'17"N 113°17'52"W). Cross Warm Springs Creek to the west side in August or later after the stream flow has decreased. Warm Springs Creek usually has strong water flows and holds brook trout with a few grayling. Hike up the west side of Warm Springs Creek 4.5 miles (7.2 km) before crossing the creek near the north side of Stewart Mountain. Follow the east fork of the stream to Stewart Lake. The total hike covers five miles (8.0 km) with an elevation gain of 400 feet (122 m).

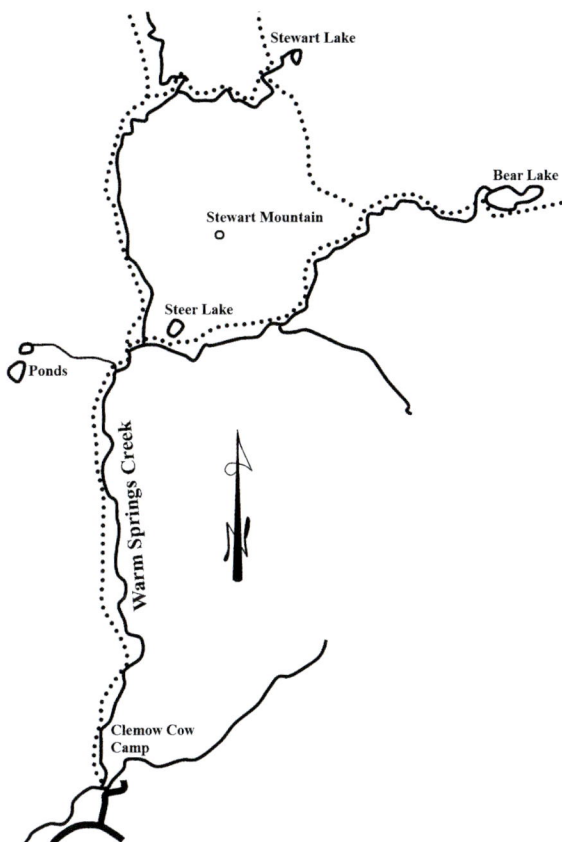

STEER LAKE

Steer Lake (45°29'45"N 113°17'25"W), really a large spring with no outlet and no fish, fills with lily pads. Located in the timber on the south side of Stewart Mountain, Steer Meadows to the east probably fills up with water during the spring providing a temporary lake. Bear Lake is two miles (3.2 km) to the east and Stewart Lake is two miles (3.2 km) to the north of Stewart Mountain. Two large ponds two miles (3.2 km) west of Steer Lake and east of Deer Peak have no fish.

FINALLY

How can a book that has been developing for 35 years be finished?

One summer as I was going into Sawtooth Lake, I met several young men and women on their way out. I knew that I was two-thirds of the way in, but to make conversation, I asked them if they could tell me how much farther the lake was. They told me that I was just beginning and that I had a long ways to go yet. They continued down the trail laughing at their joke. I had hiked into the lake long before the trail had been reconstructed, and I had used snowshoes to go into the lake about the time the young men had been born.

In some ways I wished that I did have a long ways to go, but my steps are getting slower. The book must be completed with some adventures unfinished. I must leave some future trips to the happy young men and women who I met on the trail. Maybe you could also investigate some of the places that I have missed.

The Pioneer Mountains are a special treasurer that deserves protection. The mountains are big enough to provide numerous adventures, but they are also small enough that a person could be out of the backcountry each evening if so desired.

My assignment to the reader is to enjoy the mountains and to reach timberline as often as possible. Enjoy hiking, camping, animals, birds, flowers, and the serious weather. Each person needs to provide his or her own challenges, from easy to difficult. Two mountain peaks that I would recommend would be Highboy and Sharp Mountains. I would find the easiest climbing route, but for those who are prepared, a more challenging route may be appropriate. On both mountain peaks, one should remain for a while to enjoy the area and to look for mountain goats nearby.

Chapter 6

*

WILDFLOWERS OF THE PIONEER MOUNTAINS

OLD MAN OF THE MOUNTAIN

Hiking to Crescent Lake one day,
I met the Old Man of the Mountain on the way

This Alpine Sunflower was not alone.

He and others nested close to white sandstone
Orange lichen grew on the white background.

Close by was a tree of brown
The small struggling lodgepole had been
cut back by the harsh winter wind

Arrowleaf Balsamroot grew near the ridge top
along with the Alpine Forget-Me-Not

This spot was near the top of the ridge
overlooking the Gold Creek drainage

Around the hill a Pygmy Bitterroot found
and Shooting Stars grew in marshy ground

Lake Abundance was just below
with Crescent Lake another half mile or so

Old Man of the Mountain, June 30, 2007

WILDFLOWERS

Some wildflowers bloom abundantly in certain areas, while others are uncommon to quite rare in the Pioneer Mountains. Some flowers prove easy to identify while others remain difficult.

The best areas for wildflower viewing include Vipond Park, Upper Trapper Creek, Crystal Park, Bull Creek, and Steel Creek. Most flowers grow in or near the same location year after year. Some prefer the steep wet drainages while others prefer the open hillsides or areas well above the timberline. In each of these regions, the types of flowers in bloom will change throughout the summer, and as hikers climb to higher elevations, they see flowers that bloomed at lower elevations earlier in the summer.

Vipond Park especially supports an abundance of wildflowers and varieties. Several trips beginning from mid-June through July and August would ensure varying floral shows. The type of flowers will be different beginning from Melrose, Maiden Rock, or from the town of Dewey. As you climb through the 3,000-foot (914 m) elevation change, the types of flowers will change. Also, hikers with more energy can climb the side of Black Lion Mountain to the west of Vipond Park for another 3,000-foot (914 m) elevation gain. Some arctic flowers that grow only above timberline reside on the side of Black Lion Mountain in July. Two of my favorite Arctic flowers include *Phacelia Lyallii* and Purple Saxifrage.

A few of the many flowers found in the Pioneer Mountains are discussed here.

ARROWLEAF BALSAMROOT

Arrowleaf Balsamroot has large, arrowhead-shaped leaves with smaller, sunflower-type flowers and can be found many places along roadsides and on steep ridges. The flower photographed below grew

Arrowleaf Balsamroot, June 30, 2007

near the top of the ridge in the upper Canyon Creek drainage above Canyon Lake on the trail to Abundance and Crescent Lakes.

BEARGRASS

Beargrass has many delicate small flowers that make up the main blossom. Tough, grass-like leaves surround the base. This clump of

Beargrass, July 29, 2008

leaves are the only evidence of the flower for several years until it blooms again every five to ten years. Elk, deer, and other big-game animals eat Beargrass flowers. Occasionally mice use the leaves as a nest during the winter. The Upper Lacy Creek and Baldy Lake area had numerous Beargrass stalks blooming one summer.

BITTERROOT

Bitterroot is the state flower of Montana for good reason. Its exceptionally beautiful and large pink flowers thrive on open, dry hillsides and ridgetops. Its leaves begin to grow in the fall and continues into early spring, but the leaves become smaller as the plant begins to blossom, mid- to late July at higher elevations.

Bitterroot, July 4, 2007

PYGMY BITTERROOT

Pygmy Bitterroot has some similarity to the big Bitterroot flower, but the flower is quite small, about the size of a thumbnail. Pygmy Bitterroot blooms either pink or white and has long leaves. The flower is exceptionally beautiful and would get much more attention if it were larger. It is usually found near or above timberline. An abundance of white Pygmy Bitterroot flowers can usually be found around Odell Lake in July.

Pygmy Bitterroot: Pink, July 23 and White, July 30, 2010

BLANKETFLOWER

Blanketflower, also called little sunflower, has a dark orange center.

Blanketflower, June 26, 2007

YELLOW COLUMBINE

Yellow Columbine is found in damp areas and along streams. The flower, while not abundant, can be found from low elevations through the timber to above timberline.

Yellow Columbine, August 22, 2011

ELEPHANTHEAD

Elephanthead is made up of many small elephant head-shaped flowers on a long stem. These flowers are found in very wet ground in mid-July.

Elephanthead, July 25, 2009

FAIRY SLIPPER (OR CALYPSO ORCHID)

Fairy Slipper (or Calypso Orchid) is truly a very special flower, and it is a smaller version of the larger lady's slipper. It will likely become one of your favorites. These flowers shelter in the Steel Creek drainage east of Wisdom. These orchids are uncommon to rare in the Pioneer

Mountains and should not be disturbed. Search for these treasures each year in the same location in late May through mid-June at higher elevations.

Fairy Slipper, May 30, 2009

FIREWEED

Fireweed, a tall, pink flower, grows quickly where the ground has been disturbed by excavation or by forest fires. Fireweed is especially abundant in northern Canada and Alaska and is the Yukon territorial flower.

Fireweed, August 12, 2010

GLACIER LILIES

Glacier Lilies bloom shortly after the snow melts on wet hillsides. Often millions blanket the forest. A white or cream-colored form of Glacier Lily can be found on the southwest side of the Pioneer Mountains in the Bull Creek drainage. This particular Glacier Lily is surrounded by hundreds of small, white Spring Beauties. Usually the Spring Beauty will be far more abundant than any other flower in the mountains.

Glacier Lily, June 19, 2010

HAREBELL

Harebell is a small blue bell that will become one of your favorite flowers. It usually grows among grass and other flowers at mid elevations. A smaller version grows at high elevations. In Alaska, the Harebell grows nearly twice as large with fewer flowers per plant.

Harebell, August 12, 2009

INDIAN PAINTBRUSH

Indian Paintbrush is a beautiful paintbrush-type flower found almost anyplace in the Pioneer Mountains from low elevations to alpine regions. Showing is a scarlet Paintbrush, but many color variations bloom here.

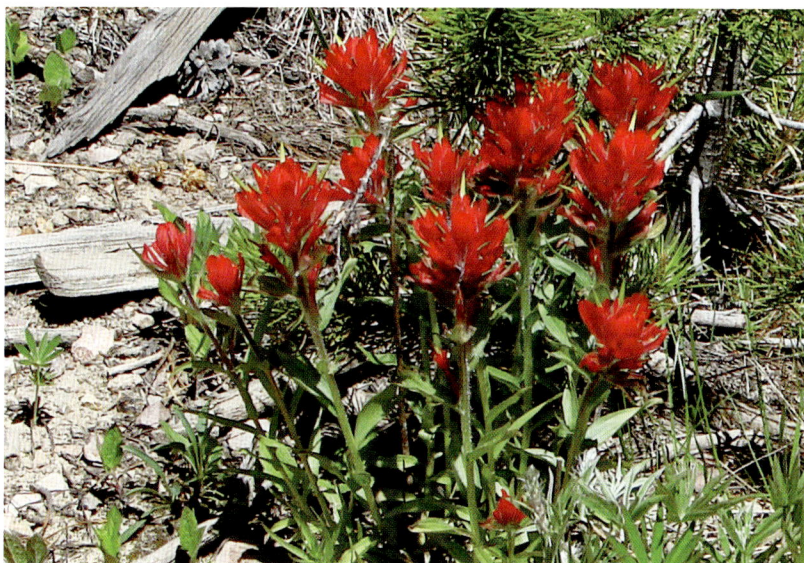

Indian Paintbrush, June 27, 2008

LUPINE

Lupine grow in open meadows and along roadsides in almost any area of the Pioneer Mountains. This group of flowers grew in the drainage north of Gorge Lakes near the top of the mountain. Notice the small lodgepole pines dwarfed by the harsh winter winds. The Lupine is truly an exceptional flower because it has a wide distribution and because it blooms from early June to the frost in mid-September. I found a white version in the Crystal Park area and a very small fuzzy version at the north end of Crystal Park.

Lupine, August, 2011

MARSH MARIGOLD

Marsh Marigold grow in wet areas in early spring. They appear near melting snow, in the snow and also under the ice. This flower was under water at Tendoy Lake, where air bubbles attached to the plant.

Marsh Marigold, July 9, 2008

MONKEYFLOWER

Monkeyflower (or Lewis Monkeyflower) scatter among other flowers in several parts of the Pioneer Mountains. This beautiful pink flower

Lewis Monkeyflower, July 7, 2007

blooms in late July and August. The yellow Monkeyflower prefers wetter areas and will usually bloom by mid-June.

PENSTEMON

Penstemon (or Penstemon-Snowlover) is a small, beautiful lavender flower that is often overlooked, yet is usually found in the timber near

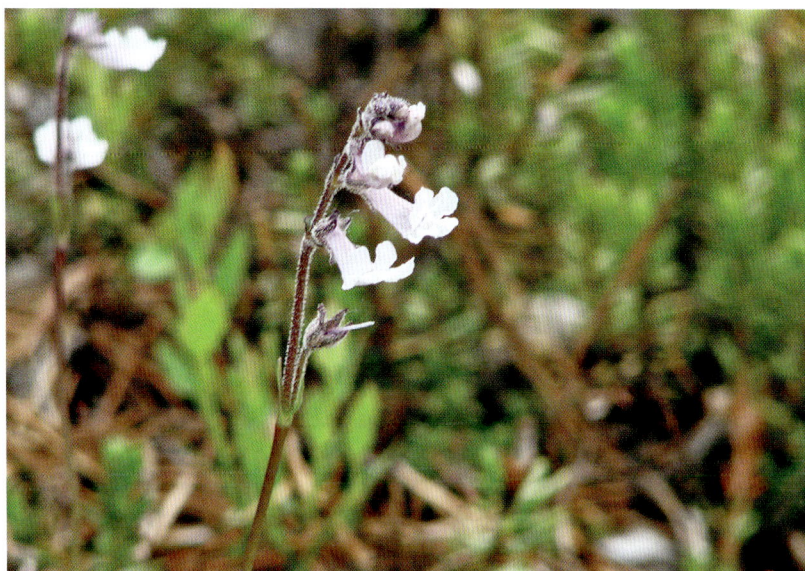

Penstemon-Snowlover, July 15, 2008

the timberline. This flower grows near both Hall and Hopkins Lakes in mid-July.

PASQUEFLOWER

Pasqueflower (or Prairie Crocus) can be abundant in the Vipond Park area in early June just after snow melts. It is the state flower of South Dakota.

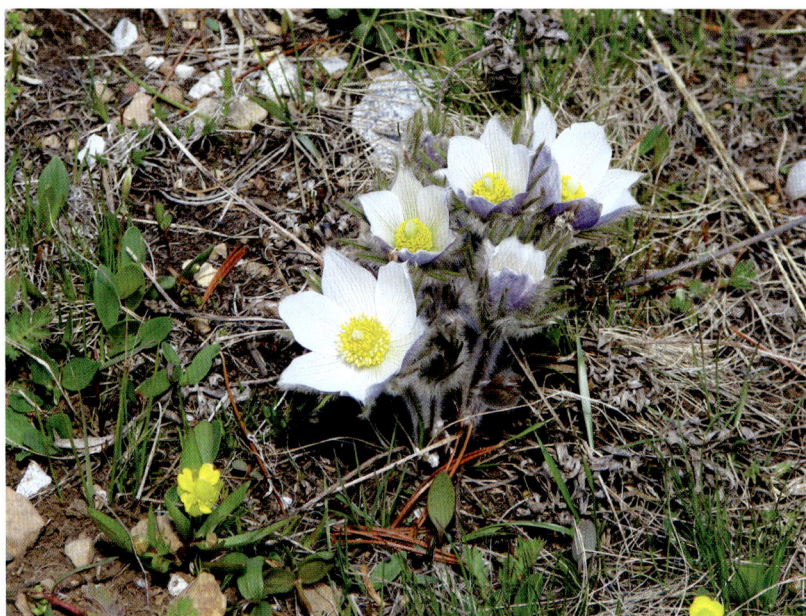

Pasqueflower, June 12, 2009

PHACELIA LYALLII

Phacelia Lyallii (or Alpine Phacelia) resides well above timberline on the east side of Black Lion Mountain just after the snow has melted. Finding this unique, brilliant blue flower will be exciting even for those who search hard for new flowers. It blooms for only a few weeks. Several other flowers endure above timberline in this same area.

Phacelia Lyallii, *July 8, 2010*

Flowers that grow above timberline have a difficult time surviving at that location, and they will probably not survive anyplace else, even with a lot of attention.

PRIMROSE

Primrose (or Tufted Evening Primrose) is a large white flower that turns pink as it ages. This flower can be found in several places west of Melrose growing in dry, barren ground.

Tufted Evening Primrose, *June 4, 2007*

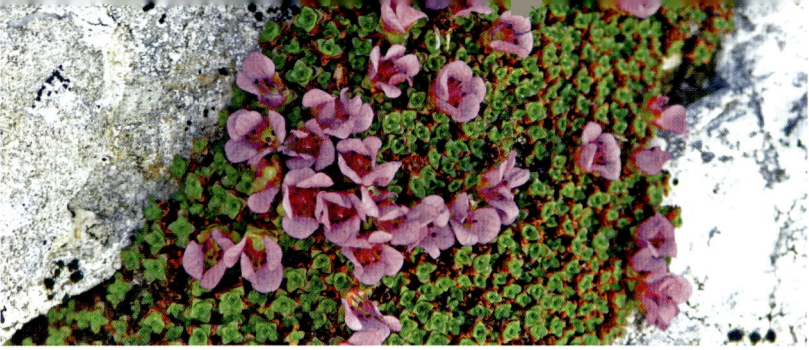

Purple Saxifrage, July 8, 2010

PURPLE SAXIFRAGE

Purple Saxifrage can be found on the east side of Black Lion Mountain in early July. This flower is the territorial flower for the Territory of Nunavut, northern Canada, and it is one of the most northern-growing flowers on earth. I imagine that the plant shown here may be older than I am and that a Purple Saxifrage may have grown in that location for several of my lifetimes. This particular flower grew on the vertical face of a rock.

PUSSYPAWS

Pussypaws can be found well above timberline, often in sand and

Pussypaws, August 30, 2011

gravel above the elevation where grass or other flowers tend to grow. This particular flower grows near Chain Lake at an elevation of 9,700 feet (2,957 m) in late August.

SEGO LILY

Sego Lily (or Mariposa Lily) can be found in late July mostly in the West Pioneer Mountains. It is the state flower of Utah.

Sego Lily, July 25, 2009

SHOOTING STAR

Shooting Star points downward like a burning meteor. It is usually purplish-pink with an occasional white variation. The Shooting Star flourishes throughout the Pioneer Mountains from early to late summer in both damp and wet ground. I have found the white Shooting Star 0.5 mile (0.8 m) downstream from Odell Lake.

Shooting Star, June 30, 2007

SWAMP LAUREL

Swamp Laurel likes wet ground and usually grows on wet banks and hillsides near alpine lakes.

Swamp Laurel, June 30, 2007

TRILLIUM

Trillium (or Wake Robin) blooms in the Steel Creek drainage east of Wisdom in early June. The western Trillium has a white flower that turns red as it matures. Larger varieties grow in the eastern United States.

Trillium, June 1, 2009

VIOLET

The Violet occurs in many varieties and it is usually found in wet areas. It may be white, yellow or blue. A small lavender Violet can be found at Stone Lake. The Yellow Mountain Violet (Goosefoot Violet) blooms in mid-June in the Steel Creek area on the hike to Proposal Rock and on the hillside above Thief Creek in the Birch Creek drainage. The Round-Leafed Yellow Violet is the more abundant variety in most areas and often blooms two weeks earlier than the Goosefoot Violet. This flower was found above Teacup Lake on a dry, windblown ridge.

The leaves of a Goosefoot Violet are shaped like a goose's foot rather than a round leaf.

Yellow Mountain Violet, July 21, 2009

Chapter 7

*

TABLES AND SELECTED REFERENCES

LAKES OF THE EAST PIONEER MOUNTAINS

	Name	Times Visited	Distance miles	Distance km	Elevation Change feet	Elevation Change meters	Hiking Difficulty	Good Fishing	Elevation feet	Elevation meters
1	Abundance Lake	13	4.9	8	1,400	430	****	***	8,750	2,670
2	Agnes Lake	6	1.6	3	800	240	*	***	7,490	2,280
3	Anchor Lake	4	6.5	10	2,000	610	****	*	9,150	2,790
4	Barb Lake	11	3.5	6	2,200	670	*****	*****	9,200	2,800
5	Black Lion Lake	1	4.5	7	2,200	670	****	*	8,780	2,680
6	Boatman Lake	8	1.4	2	100	30	**	*	8,200	2,500
7	Bobs Lake	2	4.5	7	1,700	520	***	**	8,550	2,610
8	Bond Lake	3	0.7	1	200	60	*	No	7,140	2,180
9	Bond Upper	3	6.0	10	2,300	700	****	No	9,300	2,830
10	Boot Lake	3	4.0	6	1,100	340	**	*	8,240	2,510
11	Brownes Lake	14	---	---	---	---	*	*	6,560	2,000
12	Canyon Lake	12	4.5	7	1,100	340	***	**	8,390	2,560
13	Cattle Gulch	3	3.2	5	1,200	370	**	No	8,200	2,500
14	Chain Lake	4	4.0	6	1,600	490	***	No	9,700	2,960
15	Chan Lake	3	6.5	10	1,900	580	***	No	9,020	2,750
16	Cherry Lake	18	4.2	7	1,950	590	***	*	8,820	2,690
17	Crescent Lake	13	5.5	9	1,500	460	****	****	8,790	2,680
18	Deerhead Lake	5	2.5	4	600	180	***	*	7,580	2,310
19	Dingley Lake	5	1.4	2	600	180	*	*	8,900	2,710
20	Dollar Lake	4	3.0	5	1,000	300	***	No	9,160	2,790
21	Dubois Lake	2	4.5	7	2,500	760	*****	No	9,580	2,920
22	Elkhorn Lake	5	3.7	6	1,300	400	***	**	8,700	2,650
23	Estler Lake	6	2.5	4	300	90	***	*	7,860	2,390
24	Glacier Lake	3	7.5	12	1,900	580	****	No	8,840	2,690
25	Gorge Lake (N)	14	3.2	5	1,650	500	***	***	9,150	2,790
26	Gorge Lake (S)	13	3.8	6	1,680	510	***	***	9,180	2,800
27	Grace Lake	2	3.8	6	1,570	480	****	No	8,850	2,700
28	Granite Lake	16	4.5	7	2,080	630	***	*	8,950	2,730
29	Grayling Lake	8	4.5	7	1,420	430	***	**	8,700	2,650
30	Green Lake	18	5.1	8	2,200	670	****	****	8,810	2,690

	Name	Times Visited	Distance miles	Distance km	Elevation Change feet	Elevation Change meters	Hiking Difficulty	Good Fishing	Elevation feet	Elevation meters
31	Hall Lake	11	2.0	3	900	270	***	*	8870	2700
32	Harris Lake	5	2.0	3	500	150	**	No	8650	2640
33	Hopkins Lake	11	2.0	3	900	270	***	**	8880	2710
34	Kelley Reservoir	3	0.5	1	100	30	*	*	7005	2140
35	Lily Lake East	2	3.5	5	700	210	**	No	7850	2390
36	Lion Lake	8	5.0	8	1640	500	***	**	8820	2690
37	Long Lake	3	0.2	0	50	20	*	No	7700	2350
38	Long Branch Lake	6	0.2	0	50	20	*	*	7700	2350
39	May Lake	4	5.8	9	1550	470	***	No	8700	2650
40	Minneopa Lake	14	0.3	0	80	20	*	*	8180	2490
41	Pear Lake	4	5.6	9	1550	470	***	*	8680	2650
42	Polaris Lake	2	5.5	9	1800	550	****	**	8190	2500
43	Rainbow Lake	5	1.0	2	110	30	*	**	7860	2400
44	Sawtooth Lake	5	3.0	5	1600	490	**	***	8510	2590
45	Schultz Upper	3	7.0	11	1800	550	***	**	8660	2640
46	Schultz Lower	4	6.5	10	1600	490	***	**	8500	2590
47	Scott Lake	5	4.0	6	1200	370	****	*	8700	2650
48	Tahepia Lake	3	7.6	12	2000	610	***	***	8910	2720
49	Teacup Lake	2	6.5	10	2000	610	****	No	8950	2730
50	Tendoy Lake	11	3.2	5	1200	370	**	**	9250	2820
51	Tent Lake	9	1.2	2	200	60	*	No	8380	2550
52	Torrey Lake	5	8.5	14	2000	610	****	***	8960	2730
53	Trapper Lake	4	0.2	0	100	30	*	**	8550	2610
54	Trusty Lake	3	2.0	3	800	240	**	No	7750	2360
55	Tub Lake	4	6.4	10	1950	590	***	*	9100	2770
56	Twin Lake east	8	3.0	5	700	210	**	*	8850	2700
57	Twin Lake west	8	3.0	5	700	210	**	*	8850	2700
58	Vera Lake	8	4.5	7	1420	430	***	*	8700	2650
59	Waukena Lake	7	5.0	8	1700	520	***	****	8670	2640

LAKES OF THE WEST PIONEER MOUNTAINS

	Name	Times Visited	Distance miles	Distance km	Elevation Change feet	Elevation Change meters	Hiking Difficulty	Good Fishing	Elevation feet	Elevation meters
1	Baldy Lake	4	6.5	10	1,700	520	***	**	8,560	2,610
2	Bear Lake	3	7.0	11	300	90	***	*	7,580	2,310
3	Bobcat Lake No. 1	3	3.5	6	2,000	610	***	*	8,400	2,560
4	Bobcat Lake No. 2	3	4.0	6	2,100	640	***	No	8,500	2,590
5	Bobcat Lake No. 3	3	4.3	7	2,200	670	***	No	8,420	2,570
6	Bobcat Lake No. 4	3	4.8	8	2,400	730	****	No	8,220	2,510
7	Elbow Lake	3	7.0	11	1,800	550	****	No	8,660	2,640
8	Ferguson Lake	7	2.0	3	600	180	*	***	7,530	2,300
9	Foolhen Lake	6	3.0	5	2,000	610	***	*	7,160	2,180
10	Grassy Lake	3	5.5	9	3,000	910	****	No	8,260	2,520
11	Grouse Lake 1	4	2.8	5	1,800	550	**	*	8,150	2,480
12	Grouse Lake 2	3	3.3	5	2,050	620	**	No	8,400	2,560
13	Grouse Lake 3	3	4.0	6	2,300	700	***	No	8,650	2,640
14	Johanna Lake	10	2.6	4	1,200	370	***	***	8,100	2,470
15	Lake of the Woods	5	4.5	7	1,100	340	**	*	8,450	2,580
16	Lily Lake West	6	1.5	2	700	210	*	**	7,170	2,190
17	Odell Lake	5	4.0	6	1,000	300	**	***	8,350	2,550
18	Papoose Lake	2	2.5	4	650	200	***	*	7,020	2,140
19	Sand Lake	3	5.2	8	2,450	750	****	***	8,280	2,520
20	Schwinegar Lake	8	4.4	7	1,350	410	***	***	8,220	2,510
21	Squaw Lake	2	2.8	5	600	180	***	*	7,000	2,130
22	Steer Lake	2	6.7	11	500	150	****	No	7,400	2,260
23	Stewart Lake	3	5.4	9	400	120	***	**	7,500	2,290
24	Stone Lake (W)	4	2.7	4	1,400	430	****	**	8,500	2,590
25	Stone Lake (E)	4	4.0	6	1,600	490	****	***	8,200	2,500

LAKES OF THE EAST PIONEER MOUNTAINS

	Name	Topo Quadrangle	Area in acres	Area in hectares	Depth in Feet	Depth in meters
1	Abundance Lake	Maurice Mt.	9	4	35	11
2	Agnes Lake	Storm Peak	109	44		
3	Anchor Lake	Torrey Mt., Elkhorn Hot Springs	18	7	8	2
4	Barb Lake	Torrey Mt.	13	5	50	15
5	Black Lion Lake	Vipond Park	14	6	29	9
6	Boatman Lake	Torrey Mt.	8	3		
7	Bobs Lake	Vipond Park	4	2		
8	Bond Lake	Torrey Mt., Twin Adams	10	4	12	4
9	Bond Lake (Upper)	Torrey Mt.	8	3		
10	Boot Lake	Torrey Mt.	29	12		
11	Brownes Lake	Storm Peak	38	15	25	8
12	Canyon Lake	Tahepia Mt.	10	4	9	3
13	Cattle Gulch	Cattle Gulch				
14	Chain Lake	Elkhorn Hot Springs	3	1		
15	Chan Lake	Elkhorn Hot Springs	3	1	21	6
16	Cherry Lake	Tahepia Mt.	7	3		
17	Crescent Lake	Maurice Mt.	29	12	22	7
18	Deerhead Lake	Torrey Mt.	21	8	15	5
19	Dingley Lake	Elkhorn Hot Springs	2	1		
20	Dollar Lake	Elkhorn Hot Springs, Torrey Mt.	6	2		
21	DuBois Lake	Torrey Mt.	3	1		
22	Elkhorn Lake	Elkhorn Hot Springs	10	4	25	8
23	Estler Lake	Ermont	48	19		
24	Glacier Lake	Torrey Mt.	3	1		
25	Gorge Lake (N)	Torrey Mt.	10	4	35	11
26	Gorge Lake (S)	Torrey Mt.	13	5	50	15
27	Grace Lake	Tahepia Mt.	5	2		
28	Granite Lake	Tahepia Mt.	7	3	18	5
29	Grayling Lake	Tahepia Mt.	11	4	33	10
30	Green Lake	Tahepia Mt.	24	10	92	28

LAKES OF THE EAST PIONEER MOUNTAINS

	Name	Topo Quadrangle	Area in acres	Area in hectares	Depth in Feet	Depth in meters
31	Hall Lake	Elkhorn Hot Springs	6	2	30	9
32	Harris Lake	Torrey Mt.	5	2		
33	Hopkins Lake	Elkhorn Hot Springs	12	5	45	14
34	Kelley Reservoir	Ermont	19	8		
35	Lily Lake (E)	Torrey Mt.	2	1		
36	Lion Lake	Tahepia Mt.	10	4	32	10
37	Long Lake	Tahepia Mt.	7	3	7	2
38	Long Branch Lake	Tahepia Mt.	7	3		
39	May Lake	Torrey Mt.	7	3	10	3
40	Minneopa Lake	Torrey Mt.	12	5		
41	Pear Lake	Torrey Mt.	46	19	45	14
42	Polaris Lake	Elkhorn Hot Springs	11	4		
43	Rainbow Lake	Tahepia Mt., Storm Peak	10	4	37	11
44	Sawtooth Lake	Elkhorn Hot Springs	21	8	60	18
45	Schultz (Upper)	Tahepia Mt.	7	3	12	4
46	Schultz (Lower)	Tahepia Mt.	6	2	9	3
47	Scott Lake	Polaris	7	3		
48	Tahepia Lake	Tahepia Mt.	13	5	20	6
49	Teacup Lake	Tahepia Mt.	4	2		
50	Tendoy Lake	Tahepia Mt.	22	9	100	30
51	Tent Lake	Torrey Mt.	6	2		
52	Torrey Lake	Torrey Mt.	30	12	35	11
53	Trapper Lake	Tahepia Mt.	5	2		
54	Trusty Lake	Cattle Gulch	1	0.4		
55	Tub Lake	Torrey Mt., Elkhorn Hot Springs	13	5	28	9
56	Twin Lake (E)	Torrey Mt.	4	2		
57	Twin Lake (W)	Torrey Mt.	7	3		
58	Vera Lake	Tahepia Mt.	3	1	9	3
59	Waukena Lake	Tahepia Mt.	31	13	35	11

LAKES OF THE WEST PIONEER MOUNTAINS

	Name	Topo Quadrangle	Area in acres	Area in hectares	Depth in Feet	Depth in meters
1	Baldy Lake	Stewart Mt.	28	11	85	26
2	Bear Lake	Odell Lake	14	6	25	8
3	Bobcat Lake No. 1	Odell Lake	6	2	23	7
4	Bobcat Lake No. 2	Odell Lake	5	2		
5	Bobcat Lake No. 3	Odell Lake	2	1	17	5
6	Bobcat Lake No. 4	Odell Lake				
7	Elbow Lake	Stewart Mt.	13	5	12	4
8	Ferguson Lake	Foolhen Mt.	16	6	48	15
9	Foolhen Lake	Dickie Hills	9	4	38	12
10	Grassy Lake	Odell Lake	5	2	23	7
11	Grouse Lake 1	Stine Mt.	5	2		
12	Grouse Lake 2	Stine Mt.	4	2		
13	Grouse Lake 3	Stine Mt.	4	2		
14	Johanna Lake	Foolhen Mt.	4	2		
15	Lake of the Woods	Odell Lake	10	4	30	9
16	Lily Lake (W)	Stewart Mt., Proposal Rock	14	6		
17	Odell Lake	Odell Lake	33	13	35	11
18	Papoose Lake	Shaw Mt.				
19	Sand Lake	Stewart Mt.	39	16	58	18
20	Schwinegar Lake	Odell Lake	4	2	30	9
21	Squaw Lake	Foolhen Mt.	5	2		
22	Steer Lake	Jackson Hills	1	0.4		
23	Stewart Lake	Stewart Mt.	1	0.4		
24	Stone Lake (W)	Proposal Rock	15	6	29	9
25	Stone Lake (E)	Shaw Mt.	10	4	47	14

SELECTED PIONEER MOUNTAIN PEAKS

		Elevation feet	Elevation meters
	East Pioneer Mountains		
1	Tweedy Mountain	11,154	3,400
2	Torrey Mountain	11,147	3,398
3	Granite Mountain	10,633	3,241
4	Baldy Mountain	10,568	3,221
5	Alturas Mountain No. 2	10,550	3,216
6	Barb Mountain	10,497	3,199
7	Tahepia Mountain	10,473	3,192
8	Alverson Mountain	10,467	3,190
9	Black Lion South	10,432	3,180
10	Highboy Mountain	10,431	3,179
11	Black Lion North	10,419	3,176
12	Sharp Mountain	10,357	3,157
13	Comet Mountain	10,212	3,113
14	Tent Mountain	10,193	3,107
15	Alturas Mountain No. 1	10,153	3,095
16	Sawtooth Mountain	10,144	3,092
17	Saddleback Mountain	10,118	3,084
18	Maurice Mountain	9,760	2,975
19	Sheep Mountain	9,578	2,919
20	Storm Peak	9,493	2,893
	West Pioneer Mountains		
1	Stine Mountain	9,490	2,893
2	Odell Mountain	9,405	2,867
3	Round Top Mountain	9,345	2,848
4	Alder Peak	9,197	2,803
5	Bobcat Mountain	9,165	2,793
6	Deer Peak	9,165	2,793
7	Foolhen Mountain	9,088	2,770
8	Shaw Mountain	8,950	2,728
9	Seymore Mountain	8,890	2,710
10	Maverick Mountain	8,722	2,658
11	Stewart Mountain	8,110	2,472
12	Proposal Rock	7,607	2,319

SELECTED REFERENCES

Lake and Fish Directory, Beaverhead-Deerlodge National Forest, Beaverhead-Deerlodge National Forest, 420 Barrett Street, Dillon, Montana 59724.

One Man's Dream Elkhorn Mine-Coolidge, Montana, by Shirley Wirtz Nichols and Lorene Lovell, Town & Country Publications, 1991.

The Montanans' Fishing Guide, by Dick Konizeski and updated by Dale Burk, 1982, Volume 1: West of the Continental Divide, 310 pages, Mountain Press, Missoula, Montana.

The Montanans' Fishing Guide, by Dick Konizeski and updated by Jim Derleth, 1982, Volume 2: East of the Continental Divide, 305 pages, Mountain Press, Missoula, Montana.

The Montanans' Fishing Guide, by Dick Konizeski and revised by Bill Archie and Michele Archie, Volume 1: Montana Waters West of the Continental Divide, 2001, 5th ed., 416 pages, Mountain Press, Missoula, Montana.

Wildflowers of Montana, by Donald Anthony Schiemann, Mountain Press, Missoula, Montana, 2005.

INDEX

Patricia Ann and Leroy, May 2003.

ABOUT THE AUTHOR:

I have enjoyed my forty years of teaching, retiring from Montana Tech of the University of Montana (Montana School of Mines) as a professor in General Engineering. Teaching was a great opportunity and career for me. I met many people, made many friends, and saw my students graduate and become quite successful. I hold rich memories and maintained contact with my students.

Although I have been into several mountain ranges in southwest Montana, I concentrated on hiking to every lake in the Pioneer Mountains. I have been in to several of the lakes ten to fifteen times. I especially love to hike to lakes with no trail and no fish because fewer people travel to those places, and I find solitude. I enjoy walking at the timberline where many of the lakes of the East Pioneer Mountains are located. I love to hike, to fish in the mountain lakes, to hunt in the fall, to view wildlife and wildflowers. The mountains have been my special playground.